**For coaches, teachers, parents and all those
who want to improve their game or influence others**

- Junior High School, High School
- College and Professional Golf
- Greatness
- John Wooden and his Pyramid of Success
- Teacher or Coach
- Communication
- Coaching Pointers
- Coaching Successfully
- Balancing Athletics and Academics
- Recruiting Success
- Helpful Teaching Hints
- Effective Meetings
- Key Elements for Effective Teaching
- Focus and Concentration
- Confidence
- Pressure
- How and What to Practice
- Better Approaches to Lower Scoring
- Improving Your Game
- Why People Who Work Hard Aren't Successful
- Trust and Commitment
- Athletes Get in the Zone and So Do Coaches Coaching
- Ways to Keep Your Sanity

The Wonderful World

of

Coaching Golf

by

Coach Jackie Tobian-Steinmann, UCLA

Foreword by:
John Wooden

Assistance by:
Chuck Hogan

Illustrations by:
Fritz Freeling and Walter Lantz

ISBN: 0-9726270-0-6

Printed in the United States by
Maverick Publications, Inc. • PO Box 5007 • Bend, OR 97708

Special Acknowledgment and Dedication

To Chuck Hogan, who has been a special friend and an inspiration to me during my coaching career. His words and wisdom are throughout this book.

"You're doing great," he would say. "Just keep doing the doing."

Dedication

My children, Heidi, Gregor and Lance.

They have been the light of my life. They have listened to my worries and my joys. They have always been there when I needed to talk or cry. They have followed me through all my meanderings in life with compassion and thoughtfulness. I cannot imagine ever having to go through life without them. I am a lucky mother to have three magnificent children, and so this book is dedicated to them.

Friends Who Assisted Me
Throughout My Years of Coaching

This book is the result of years of coaching and information gathered from many people, many books, many seminars and many mistakes and successes. Here is a partial list of people who have helped me along the way:

Lynn Marriott - LPGA Teacher and Lecturer
Pia Nilsson - Teacher and Former Swedish Team Coach
David Witt - PGA
Chuck Hogan - Author and Lecturer
Renee Baumgartner, Ph.D. - Senior Athletic Director,
    University of Oregon
Dr. James V. Durlacker, Ph.D. - Author
Mark Lasch - Golf Stat
Therese Hession - Ohio State University Coach
Dan Brooks - Duke University Coach
Dianne Dailey -Wake Forest University Coach
Ken Keneda - PGA Teacher and HG Club Fitter
Bruce, Randy and Ross Henry - Henry Griffiths Golf Clubs
Rich Bertolucci - Sports information - UCLA
Betsy Clarke, Ph.D. - LPGA Vice President of Professional
    Development
Kerry Graham – Former President of the LPGA Teaching
    Division and Lecturer
All the Coaches at UCLA
And many other coaches too numerous to mention.

I always liked a statement made by Chuck Hogan, and it is true. "I screw up less people than I used to." Therefore, use this book as you like. Copy the information and give it to your students. Use your imagination and change anything or everything. Enjoy!

Something to Think About

It's a funny thing about life;
If you refuse to accept
anything but the best,
you very often get it.

Somerset Maugham

Table of Contents

Something to Think About

It's what you learn after you know it all that counts.

John Wooden

Foreword

After many years of experience and countless hours of research, coach Jackie Steinmann has come up with a book that is entitled *The Wonderful World of Coaching Golf*. In reality, it is a book that reaches far beyond coaching. From my own personal review, I honestly feel that it is not just a book about golf or any other sport; it is a book about how to succeed in life. It will teach the many prerequisites needed to execute one's peak level of competency whether it be in the game of golf or the game of life.

Our culture values sports. Sports have a meaningful role in society. Athletes are role models, whether they want to be or not. They are a reflection of our society in terms of their behavior. Coaches are teachers who should focus on building character and, in many ways, that is what this book is about.

I would recommend that all parents read this book. I am quite confident that they would find many things to help them work with children in sports as well as in other areas of their lives. I also believe that coaches and teachers in any sport should use this book as a reference guide. The wisdom found here will help make coaching more fun, creative and productive for both the coach and the athlete.

Coach John Wooden

Preface

Amusing as this drawing might seem, it is what most amateur golfers think when they address the ball and play the game. How about you? What are you thinking?

From its inception golf, in particular, has taken a mechanical approach unlike other sports. Being mentally prepared is unfamiliar to the majority of golfers and is the last thing they are concerned about when warming up, competing or just playing a friendly game. For the majority of golfers, mechanics of the swing is probably the most prevalent thing on their minds. If it isn't working, it must be the fault of their mechanics or swing. Therefore, golfers are always in a revolving circle of fix-the-mechanics. This cycle can be attributed to the way golf has been taught since teachers entered the picture. I don't believe the Scots, who originated the game, wondered at any time about the mechanics of how to get a leather ball around the fields and hills and into a dirt hole with their makeshift clubs.

Golf has come a long way since the early 1800's. Much money is now connected with success in golf, and people are constantly in search of the perfect swing.

The mechanics of the swing play an important part in learning the skills of golf. This, of course, is a necessity at the beginning of the learning process. Mechanics, however, must be learned quickly, habituated and then forgotten. As we get better and better at playing the game there are small changes, mechanically, that we can make to improve our performances when what we are doing is not working. Golf is really an easy game if you prepare yourself both mentally and physically. It is the teachers, coaches, and the golfers themselves, with some of their limiting beliefs, who make it difficult.

We all know that golf is a game, but how many people actually play the game? Most people play the game of *golf swing*. Think about it. **Do you go for a lesson in playing the game or do you go to get a lesson in golf swing?** I would like to believe that you could look at a good golf swing, emulate it, and then do it, maybe not accurately the first few times, but better and better the more you watch and the more you emulate.

I have a young grandson who was in Little League baseball as a boy and learned golf this way: I demonstrated what the golf swing looked like. I gave him a club that was about right for his size, showed him the baseball hold and the athletic position. I told him to wind up and go to the finish position. **"Presto! Automagicly!"** That was all the instruction he needed. I gave him custom clubs that fit him, courtesy of Henry Griffiths, and in no time he was shooting in the seventies, with no more lessons other than what to do and how to behave on the golf course.

My grandson's swing was not mechanically perfect but naturally good, and he got better and better the more he watched and imitated. Since then, he has learned and improved by watching good players and playing golf. Henry Griffiths lengthened his clubs as he grew. He is sixteen years old now, hits it a mile, is on the high school golf team and loves it. I think there is much to be learned from children. Just watching them succeed offers many lessons. Our beliefs about how hard the sport of golf is would definitely lessen or disappear, if we could all learn as children do.

Most of my coaching career has been involved with assisting players in mental preparation. I have left the mechanics to the mechanic teachers. My biggest challenge as a coach was to get athletes to put the mechanics away when playing the game. There remains much to be done to re-educate people so that they can rediscover their imagination, creativity and have fun playing the game of golf.

This book is about incorporating mental techniques into the learning process for teachers, coaches, parents and golfers like you. This is not a book of swing mechanics. It is about coaching *after* swing mechanics, using ideas and proven methods developed over a period of many years of coaching. This book is for parents of budding golfers, for high school and college coaches, for professional teachers and for anyone interested in coaching him/herself to become a better player of the game. The book is intended to be an easy to read, all-inclusive source of information for achieving greater success in any sport. The book offers other ways of learning, playing, and communicating that are critical to maximizing success.

I always knew that I would be a teacher. I loved sharing my experiences and assisting others. As long as I can remember, I have been teaching somebody something. I sought experts, attended clinics, seminars and took many self-improvement courses. During my coaching career, I learned from the best in the field, read many books and experimented with numerous ideas. I loved being around people who were successful, and I learned from them. Later in my coaching career, I started assisting the new coaches in the country by sharing my coaching philosophy and ideas. This book is for the coaches I know, the coaches I have not met and for all coaches everywhere in any sport.

There is magic inside all of us just waiting to be discovered.

Jackie Tobian-Steinmann

Education
Undergraduate - AB Degree in Zoology from UCLA
Graduate Degree in Art as Applied to Medicine from the
    University of Toronto
California State General Secondary Teaching Credential
Professional Ski Instructor - Certified WPSIA-PSIA
LPGA Teaching Professional - Class A, Life Member

Accomplishments in Collegiate Golf
43 Tournament Victories
227 Top Ten Finishes
5 Pac 10 Championships Titles
Runner up at National Championships - 1990
National Championship Title - 1991
4th place National Championships-1996
Many All-Americans and Academic All-Americans

Honors
Life Membership LPGA
Honorary Membership in the Professional Ski Instructors of America
Honorary Membership Valencia Women's Golf Club
Honorary Membership Wilshire Country Club
Founder and President of the National Golf Coaches Association
Western Section LPGA Coach of the Year - 1987, 1992
LPGA Coach of the Year - 1990
Pac 10 Coach of the Year - 1983, 1984, 1985, 1990, 1991
Regional Coach of the Year - 1983, 1984, 1991, 1996
Nominated for National Coach of the Year - 1986, 1988, 1996
National Coach of the Year - 1996

Taylor Made National Coach of the Year - 1991

Inaugural Rolex Gladys PalmerMeritotorius Award - 1987
for contribution to Collegiate Golf

Inducted into the Collegiate Golf Hall of Fame - 1989

Coach of the U.S. College Golf Team 1992

Chairman of the 1996 National NCAA Golf Championships - 1996

Rolex Gladys Palmer Meritotorious Award-1999 for contribution to
Collegiate Golf

Lifetime Achievement Award - 1999

Steinmann Endowment for Golf at UCLA

Steinmann Scholarship for Coaches in the National Golf
Coaches Association

Something to Think About

There is a story about God and three angels in which God says to the angels, "Where shall we hide the secret of life? One angel replies by proposing that it should be buried in the depths of the ocean, but God said, "No, with modern technology it would be found fairly fast." The next angel proposes that it should be hidden on the highest mountain, to which God replies, "No, where there is a mountain, it will be climbed and explored and the secret will be found." The third angel says, "I know, let's hide the secret of life inside each individual." And God replies, "I think you've got it, no one will think of looking there!"

CHAPTER I

Introduction

HOW IT USED TO BE
THE OLDEST WOMEN'S INTERCOLLEGIATE SPORT [1]

In the old days, the players' equipment rooms were the trunk and the back seat of their coach's car, an old Ford which doubled as the team bus. Their training table meals usually consisted of cold cereal, trail mix, low-fat milk, and a packed lunch because they were always trying to save money.

A group of traveling, would-be collegiate Andrew sisters, you say? A busload of excited chorus girls and a voice coach? Don't believe it! In the day of liberated ladies and equal facilities for men's and women's collegiate athletics, this was how the first women's golf team at UCLA got ready for each match.

Led by their coach, a determined redhead, the team was not exactly coddled, courted or heavily subsidized. Although their quarters, which they shared with several other coaches, was a 3-wood away from the main athletic facilities, it might as well have been in the boonies. Golf was a minor sport and not high on the totem pole of most administrations still affected by the cruel budget cuts of Proposition 13.

Thus, in the halcyon days for name collegiate athletes, the members of the golf team remained anonymous. With the exception of a few basketball stars, collegiate women pursued their individual sport *incognito*. Technically they existed, but institutional support and media coverage was meager. Actually, the press was not at fault. Although hundreds of thousands of dollars were made available and spent for men's sports, particularly basketball and football, because of their spectator appeal, not much was left for women's activities, especially golf, where ticket sales were not a factor.

If the golf team needed uniforms, the coach persuaded manufacturers to supply them free. In order to find places to practice, endless hours were spent writing "please" and "thank you" letters to various country clubs around the town, even though women were allowed to play only at certain times, usually before 7:00 a.m. and after 5:00 p.m. However, the players considered themselves lucky to be able to play on such prestigious golf courses. Unlike baseball or basketball, golf teams could not use the neighborhood gym, parking lot or Little League field. Yet, practice was a must and the teams used those courses for competition.

As golf emerged onto the collegiate scene, some colleges took women's golf very seriously and backed up their programs with substantial funds. Other schools then had to do the same, if they were going to compete, especially colleges that had high scholastic standards but did not offer scholarships to promising athletes who were not *bona fide* students.

Fundraising venues such as college-amateur events became popular because the money generated benefited the golf teams and helped colleges to be competitive. Thanks to the generosity of many local country clubs and their members, the coaches were able to find enough places to play and publicity began to focus on college golf. Some celebrities and business people were sympathetic and simply made time in their busy schedules to help out and lend the prestige of their names to the fund-raising tournaments. Their efforts usually paid dividends. The golf events usually surprised everyone as they successfully raised money for scholarships, equipment and travel.

Coaches consistently looked out for good junior golfers. They knew that the women's professional champions of tomorrow would come from the ranks of collegiate golfers. Therefore, if they wanted to see exciting new faces on the tour, supporting collegiate golf teams was necessary.

So as you drove the freeways or highways in those days, if you happened to see a van loaded down with pretty young women in school colors, with maybe a redhead at the wheel, singing at the top of their voices, golf clubs sticking out the windows, the interior bulging with bags, briefcases and brown paper bag lunches, it just might not have been a small band of gypsies, but rather a golf team on its way to a championship.

---

[1] Adapted from article written by Joe Mizrahi.

HISTORY OF THE UCLA GOLF TEAM

The UCLA Women's Golf Team began as a five-player team, in 1976, with the hiring of part time coach Jackie Tobian-Steinmann. As an AIAW sport, tournaments were usually local one-day events. Occasionally there were some three-day events.

UCLA competed in its first National Championship in 1978, and as the program improved it gained top recruits, which meant success. It was a surprise to everyone in 1979 when UCLA came in fifth at the National Championships at the University of Georgia.

Each year the program got better. Practice facilities donated by the local country clubs, *i.e.* Los Angeles Country Club, Brentwood Country Club, Hillcrest Country Club, Bel Air Country Club, Riviera Country Club, Mountain Gate Country Club, Wilshire Country Club and Vista Valencia Golf Course made a big difference.

In 1978, the AIAW was abolished and the NCAA took over. UCLA continued to improve and slowly became one of the best in the country. In 1990 UCLA was runner-up at the National Championships, and in 1991 they were crowned the National Champions in an exciting playoff with San Jose State University. UCLA remained consistently in the top ten and many times in the top five nationally. Coach Steinmann remained its leader until 1999, and only the players changed. The program and its reputation gained prominence worldwide and to this day remains a national contender. Over the years, UCLA players have come from Sweden, England, Scotland, Denmark, France, Italy, and Switzerland, and there have been many Japanese, Korean, and Taiwanese Americans. Teams have reflected a worldwide atmosphere, which has attributed to its prosperity. Many of the team members have gone on to the professional tours, or entered the corporate world.

With all of the above, the future and success of UCLA Women's Golf remains constant because of the philosophy and goals of Coach Steinmann. Her leadership in Women's Golf has been rewarded with Hall of Fame Honors, twice the Rolex Gladys Palmer Award for her contribution to Collegiate Golf, and many Coach of the Year awards. She was the originator of the National Golf Coaches Association and its first president.

Coach Steinmann retired in June of 1999, and in September the team was turned over to the very capable new coach, Carrie Leary, who was a former UCLA golfer and a member of the 1991 Championship team. Her leadership was rewarded with a fifth place finish at the 2001 NCAA Championships.

Something to Think About

No written word
No spoken plea
Can teach our youth
What they should be.
Nor all the books
On all the shelves.
It's what the teachers
Are themselves.

To all parents:
Something to Think About

JUNIOR HIGH SCHOOL, HIGH SCHOOL, COLLEGE AND PROFESSIONAL GOLF

Most children cannot handle instruction before the age of seven. Parents who want their children to learn to play golf should expose children to golf by example. Let them watch, and let them enjoy the fun of pretending to be a golfer. As children get older and show interest in the sport, opportunity to experiment and having fun should be the primary consideration. They should play golf only because they want to.

Realizing that opportunities are still limited for many young golfers, the mentality is changing largely because of Tiger Woods, well-meaning professionals, the LPGA, the PGA, facility owners and equipment companies.

There are big steps to take between junior golf and college golf and then professional golf. Sometimes they are monumental. Young golfers are getting better and better. They are more athletic, playing golf with outstanding skills and hitting the ball farther. They are playing with better equipment, getting better instruction, and even having professionals and mental coaches caddying for them in tournaments. Maybe not all this attention and life style is good for young players. Pressure sometimes has a way of developing serious behavior problems.

Even so, junior golfers are on the increase and with this surge certain unique problems are occurring with alarming frequency. Many juniors are showing behavioral tendencies that display poor sportsmanship. Who is responsible? Being taught to act like an adult when they are young may be the problem. The unacceptable behavior on and off the golf course could stem from an emphasis on winning too early in childhood. Are they being pampered and catered to, spoiled and over-trained? Are parents and coaches pushing them to win too much? Are these adults good role models for our young people? These questions are vital questions in the success and future of our youth. Here are the headlines in the *L.A. Times*, June 26, 2001:

Adults Brawl After Boys Soccer Match; 2 Hurt
Violence: Three are arrested as more than 30
parents and coaches clash...

Role models?

Attitudes need to change about sports and the importance of winning in our culture today. However, in defense of young people, the good news about learning and playing golf and other sports is that they are activities that take a great deal of time, keep kids off the streets and associate them with other young people with whom they can compete and develop friendships that will last a lifetime.

High school golf is the training ground for college golf, and college golf is a training ground for professional golf, and the same problems occur. High school and college coaches have a great responsibility to educate young golfers in acceptable behavior and guide them in making good decisions. Many high schools have good golf programs. Girls' golf is on the increase, but most girls play on the boys' golf teams. High school golf coaches have many responsibilities and teaching assignments. It is difficult for high school coaches to devote enough time to coaching.

Some college coaches have academic teaching assignments also, but full time coaching is the norm in most Division I universities. They also have recruiting responsibilities, and do most of their recruiting of junior athletes in their senior year. The pressure of the recruiting process is sometimes overwhelming, and the objectives unrealistic. High school seniors, in my opinion, are pressured many times to obtain scholarships for the wrong reasons. In the 1990's, the scholarship award system got out of hand. Some parents and coaches treat scholarships like a corporate decision. They scrutinize universities, college coaches, teams and athletes as if the university owed them a scholarship. It is important to investigate scholarship criteria and examine all the possibilities, but manipulation is a poor way to get something and it certainly is not a good example for young people and parents to exhibit. However, a scholarship awarded to a deserving young athlete is a rewarding experience for both coach and athlete.

Athletes should attend a university where they feel comfortable with the coach and the team. This should be their prime consideration. Money may be a big concern, but if an athlete is unhappy, the money won't help and success is definitely undermined. Many grants and loans are available, as well as academic scholarships. These should be investigated if money is a problem. The public library is a good place to start. Even after entering college, students can earn scholarships. Most coaches in college will reward the best athletes with scholarship opportunities. (Note. In Chapter II, On Recruiting, there is an example of how much money a Division I University spends on a scholarship athlete over a period of four years, as well as information on getting into a university.)

Entering the world of professional golf is a giant step attempted by many and awarded to few. Professional golf is a tough road at the very best. It takes demanding determination that must be mustered for long periods. I believe the statistic of successful golfers reaching the professional level is less than one percent. That is not a very big percentage. Maturity is probably the most important quality. Being able to handle the rigors of professional life is not all that glamorous. No longer are you looked after, given everything, and told how to handle day-to-day living as you were in college. Professionally the emphasis is on you alone. You take care of you, and everybody else is out there to beat your butt. Having the money to make it professionally is the big concern for many players. Perceived as a glamorous world, it takes exceptional skills and personalities. Chasing your dreams is commendable, but your years in college are some of the most important and fun years of your life. The college experience will give you the maturity to realize your dreams and accomplish your goals. In most cases, it is the more mature and veteran golfers who are successful on the professional tours.

JOHN WOODEN

John Wooden, at age 93 as of this writing, is one of the most successful coaches of all time. He not only won ten national championships in a row at UCLA, but he was instrumental in the molding of many athletes, some who changed their lives dramatically and forever. He was a teacher of life, love and the pursuit of success. He shaped players into successful human beings and was a true model of his philosophy.

No book with the emphasis on success could be published without including legendary coach Wooden's Pyramid of Success. There are many lessons that can be taught from each section. Use your imagination.

Coach Wooden was an inspiration to me in my coaching career. Sitting next to me early in my career at a banquet, he said, "Never try to be better than someone else, Jackie, always be the best that you can be." I will never forget that advice. Later in my career, when I started dreaming about the book I wanted to write, I asked him some questions and the following were his answers.

What is your profession? Dumb question when I think of it now.
I am a teacher of English, basketball, baseball and tennis.

What advice would you give to beginning coaches?
Follow the Pyramid of Success from bottom to top beginning with the cornerstones, industriousness, enthusiasm, and all you can find in books, videos, *etc.* in regard to your profession. Look for common threads among all those you respect and admire. Learn the laws of learning and how to apply them.

What is your philosophy?
The Golden Rule.

What has been the most successful part of you coaching?
Almost all of my players graduated and have done well in their chosen professions. Also being a teacher.

What has been your greatest challenge in coaching?
Getting my players to keep winning and losing in proper perspective. Teaching them that you never lose when you have made the effort to do the best of which you are capable.

What advice would you give to coaches and athletes alike?
Do not expect to start at the top, but look for opportunities to work with those who excel.

How have you handled unacceptable behavior?
Denying the privilege of practicing and playing. Correct problems as they occur and do it with tact without antagonizing. Do not harp on the past.

What do you consider the most important factor in success?
Being prepared to execute near your own level of competency. Failure to prepare in preparing to fail.

How have you created a balance for your student athletes?
100% concentration at practice, but teaching them that they are a student the rest of the time with a reasonable amount of time for social activities. Leave basketball on the floor.

What do you look for when recruiting student athletes?
1. Intelligence
2. Quickness in relation to others who play the same position.
3. Team attitude of unselfish play and consideration for others.
4. Self-control

An interesting question I asked was: What do you consider an equitable process for tournament qualifying? (Note: I was thinking golf, he was thinking basketball. In a way, considering some politics these days, the answer could apply to both.)
Winning your conference and not being voted in.

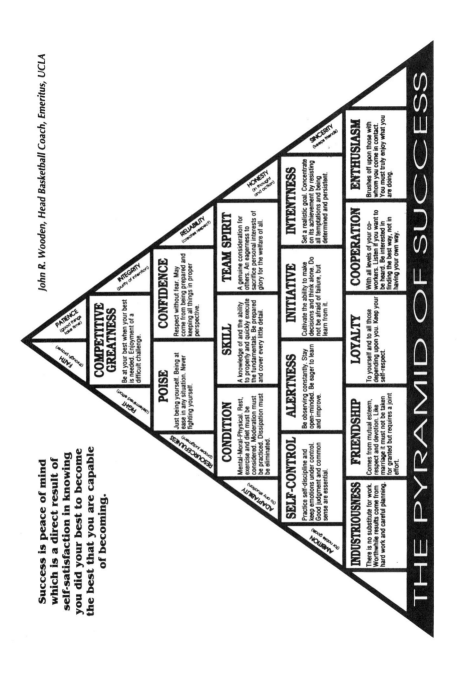

Success is peace of mind which is a direct result of self-satisfaction in knowing you did your best to become the best that you are capable of becoming.

John R. Wooden, Head Basketball Coach, Emeritus, UCLA

THE PYRAMID OF SUCCESS

FAITH (through prayer)

PATIENCE (good things take time)

COMPETITIVE GREATNESS
Be at your best when your best is needed. Enjoyment of a difficult challenge.

INTEGRITY (purity of intention)

CONFIDENCE
Respect without fear. May come from being prepared and keeping all things in proper perspective.

POISE
Just being yourself. Being at ease in any situation. Never fighting yourself.

RIGHT (of heart sense)

RELIABILITY (creates respect)

TEAM SPIRIT
A genuine consideration for others. An eagerness to sacrifice personal interests or glory for the welfare of all.

SKILL
A knowledge of and the ability to properly and quickly execute the fundamentals. Be prepared and cover every little detail.

CONDITION
Mental-Moral-Physical. Rest, exercise and diet must be considered. Moderation must be practiced. Dissipation must be eliminated.

RESOURCEFULNESS (proper judgment)

HONESTY (in thought and action)

INTENTNESS
Set a realistic goal. Concentrate on its achievement by resisting all temptations and being determined and persistent.

INITIATIVE
Cultivate the ability to make decisions and think alone. Do not be afraid of failure, but learn from it.

ALERTNESS
Be observing constantly. Stay open-minded. Be eager to learn and improve.

ADAPTABILITY (to any situation)

SINCERITY (keeps friends)

ENTHUSIASM
Brushes off upon those with whom you come in contact. You must truly enjoy what you are doing.

COOPERATION
With all levels of your co-workers. Listen if you want to be heard. Be interested in finding the best way, not in having your own way.

LOYALTY
To yourself and to all those depending upon you. Keep your self-respect.

FRIENDSHIP
Comes from mutual esteem, respect and devotion. Like marriage it must not be taken for granted but requires a joint effort.

SELF-CONTROL
Practice self-discipline and keep emotions under control. Good judgment and common sense are essential.

INDUSTRIOUSNESS
There is no substitute for work. Worthwhile results come from hard work and careful planning.

AMBITION (for noble goals)

Something to Think About

GREATNESS

It is easy to be great because great people are there to assist you. Wherever I go, I find people who are willing to share their ideas. The successful coaches/teachers will share their secrets. They are always willing to give the new or struggling coach/player helpful hints or new ideas. Find these people, seek them out, write them, call them on the phone and read what they say.

If you want to be successful, hang around with successful people.

Something to Think About

The best coaches are the ones who realize not only what works in coaching, but also why it works.

CHAPTER II

Coaching Responsibilities

TEACHER OR COACH

The differences between a coach and a teacher are subtle, but there are differences. Everyone who plays golf is a teacher, and even the people who don't play golf are teachers. A teacher is someone who tells you what to do or how to do it. This is true in any sport, but in golf, you just have to wander up and down a driving range and listen to the instruction being given by various people short and tall. Boyfriends teach girlfriends, fathers teach daughters, grandmas teach grandchildren, husbands teach wives, and golf instructors teach everybody. Sometimes it is good advice and sometimes it is not so good.

Coaches are generally more nurturing. They are also teachers in that they assist or guide people to achieve success. Coaching takes great understanding and awareness of how people learn for students to learn effectively. A good coach is more interested in the *what* and *why* of success and is able to assist people in that direction.

The biggest difference between a coach and a teacher is, teachers teach what they want you to know and coaches teach what the student wants to know. Generally speaking, the teacher gives technical information, the coach helps the student increase awareness. This having been said, I want you to know that this book is not about teaching swing mechanics. This book is about coaching people through the experience of golf and how to use that experience in their lives.

Coaches in all arenas have great responsibility. On their shoulders lie the future of our youth and the future of golf. If you are a mother, father, teacher or coach, this book can inspire you and maybe make you think a little. No matter what, you can't go wrong if you offer unconditional love and acceptance whether they win or lose, and have rules that are clear, concise, fair and true for everybody. You are the model.

Chuck Hogan expressed it concisely in his article *The Coach.* "All athletic activity should be a win for the child. The child can learn this only from the model, the coach. The child is interested in playing and participation. The child will play as long as the game is fun. The game must be kept a game. The desire to win is an adult idea, which can have disastrous consequences. Even though the coach, teacher, parent has the best of intentions, the child quickly learns the meaning of losing and how it feels to be a loser. This concept can be devastating and can influence the rest of a child's life." I might add from my experience, that this seems to be true for everyone in any endeavor at any age.

Something to Think About

Golf is about life. Watch someone play golf and you will know how he or she runs their life and what they think about themselves.

PHILOSOPHY

The dictionary defines philosophy as "a system for guiding life as a body of principles of conduct or traditions." "A philosopher is a thinker who builds a system, lives in accordance with a set of philosophical principles, and meets difficulties serenely and intelligently."[2]

It is important that every teacher and coach has a set of principles to live by. Thinking about what you believe and what you know works, from your experience and the experiences of successful people, guides you in your daily life. Knowing what you want and what you believe can assist you in being a great model. Included below are beliefs, used for teaching and coaching at UCLA. These may give you some ideas for forming your own philosophy.

UCLA GOLF PURPOSE AND PHILOSOPHY
By Jackie Tobian-Steinmann: Head Golf Coach 1976-1999

The goal of the UCLA golf program is to be a leader in Women's Golf. We have a vision to make the world a better place by just being in it, and being the best that we can be with dignity, charity and respect.

Our objectives are:
To provide each student with the best education possible and encourage them to graduate from the University.
To have each athlete perform as her very best, continue to improve and in the process have fun and enjoy the experience of challenging golf.
To make College rewarding and memorable.

---

[2] *World Book Encyclopedia* dictionary, p. 1458.

We believe:

The experience of being a team player will assist them the rest of their life.

There are no limitations, each individual has unlimited potential.

Everyone is special and has their own way of doing what works best for them.

Camaraderie, loyalty and pride in the University are important, as well as, compassion responsibility and self-respect.

Attitude determines aptitude.

There is no such thing as failure, only an outcome and discovering another way to accomplish something.

Each person should be safe fast and courteous on the golf course so that they are not intimidated.

Discipline and success go hand in hand.

Learning good habits will assist us in getting what we want.

In developing priorities, goals and communication skills.

In the benefits of nutrition and physical fitness.

In eliminating interferences that prevent us from achieving.

In having each athlete club fitted by experts so that their equipment rewards their swing.

In learning how to aim and align.

The short game is the primary discipline to lower scores. We "Aim to Win"[3] by being the best putters we can possible be.

In staying competitive by playing with the best.

In learning the rules of golf.

In learning the most effective ways to practice.

In learning to emphasize target orientation through imagination.

In learning team building and characteristics of highly effective teams.

In continuing to develop mechanical expertise in a rewarding way.

In learning how to become competent and confident.

In penetrating barriers and learning to be adaptable.

In learning from successful people and welcoming new ideas.

In acting, walking, talking and looking like winners.

In learning to get emotionally attached to the good shots and unemotionally attached to the bad shots.

In discovering each individual's learning style, behavior patterns, biases and style of communication so that we can discover the best way to guide each individual.

---

[3] Chuck Hogan.

We encourage:

Players to play for their reasons and not for somebody else's reason.

Each student athlete to be the best that they can be instead of trying to be better than somebody else.

Athletes to dream big dream, and become their vision.

GOLF IS ONLY ... JUST A GAME.

Cannot be reprinted or distributed without consent of UCLA.

NEURO-LINGUISTIC PROGRAMMING

Modeling and doing what successful people do is a great way to learn. Using already successful methods observed in others is a way to teach, parent or coach.

Neuro-Linguistic Programming or **NLP**, founded by John Grinder and Richard Bandler, is a method of studying people and how they excel athletically, professionally and personally. **Neurons** are part of the nervous system. They govern our five senses. **Linguistics** comes from the word communication. **Programming**, in this sense, is the way we choose to organize ideas and actions to produce results.

Successful people have specific ways of doing things. They take advantage of their choices, and what they truly believe and think about happens. The more choices you have the more chance you have to succeed. Successful people understand that being adaptable is necessary for making better or different choices, and they usually discover and become aware of what works best for them.

Therefore, if we mold ourselves after successful people and we work toward our goals, success should happen. Right? Sometimes yes and sometimes no. What we think we want and what we spend our time focusing on may be two different things. For example, if an athlete says, "I want to be the best putter in the country," and you observe him always working on the driving range, then you can quickly ascertain that being the best putter is not really, what he wants.

A very provocative statement from NLP is the following:

"If you always do what you've always done, you'll always get what you've always got. If what you are doing is not working, do something else." [4]

---

[4] *Introducing NLP*, Joseph O'Connor and John Seymour, p. 9, 1990.

You cannot imagine how many times this quote has made people reflect. They usually laugh because it really hits home.

There are many books on the subject of NLP. One of the best is *Introducing NLP* written by Joseph O'Connor and John Seymour. It is essential reading for any teacher, coach or parent. You can learn how to communicate better, develop leadership qualities, earn respect and assist people in discovering how to succeed.

NLP PRESUPPOSITIONS[5]

The following set of useful assumptions about people and the world are NLP presuppositions. They may not be all "true" in every case, but acting as if they were true is very useful.

- The map is not the territory. We all have different maps of the world. No map reflects the world completely and accurately.
- Mind and body affect each other.
- The meaning of communication is the response you get.
- Resistance is a comment about the communicator.
- If what you are doing is not working, do anything else.
- People make the best possible choices with the information they have.
- The part with the most adaptability will be the most controlling part in a system.
- Behind every behavior is a positive intention.
- There is no failure, only feedback. If something does not work, you can utilize that as feedback and try anything else.
- If one person can learn to do something, anyone else can.
- People work perfectly. No one is broken.
- Every behavior is useful in some context.
- Choice is better than no choice.
- People have the ability to use all the sources they need.
- Anything can be accomplished if the task is taken in small enough chunks.

---

[5] Adapted from Chuck Hogan, S.E.A., Inc. 1989.

APPLIED KINESIOLOGY

The pioneer of Applied Kinesiology was Dr. George J. Goodheart, Jr. His experiments and research attracted many psychologist and physicians. Among them was Dr. James V. Durlacher. *Freedom from Fear Forever* written by Dr. Durlacker is an easy way to understand the process of applied kinesiology. He calls it Acu-power. It is a method of determining what people really believe. We know that everything you have ever done or learned from inception through your whole life is recorded in your nervous system—every fear, anxiety, pleasure, every taste, sensation, and everything you have seen or heard. These records can be threatening or non-threatening and can produce pain or pleasure when we think about them. We always move toward pleasure and away from pain. Sometimes we try to do both at the same time, which causes problems like the yips.

Using Acu-power is simply a way of testing a specific muscle for strength while the person is thinking of a fear or uncomfortable situation. If a belief is positive, the muscle is strong. If a belief is unsure or completely negative, the muscle is weak. Anyone can learn this technique. It is a simple procedure and can be learned easily from reading his book. Using the arm-testing procedure at a tournament a coach, for example, could discover if athletes were ready to play, if they believed that they could play well and deserved to play well. Fears could be detected that prevented them from excelling, and beliefs could be changed. Learning and using the principles of educational kinesiology will allow you to be a better golfer, teacher, coach or parent.

In *Quantum Healing*, Deepak Chopra, MD, explains how people have boundaries which prevent them from achieving their goals. Many golfers are either open ended or limiting themselves as they are tested with Dr. Durlacker's procedure of muscle testing. This test enables a coach to be aware of each athlete's beliefs. This method also gives a coach procedures to help change their beliefs. *Freedom from Fear Forever* is a must-read for coaches, teachers and parents.

Adapted from book "Freedom from Fear Forever" by Dr. Durlacker

BRICK WALLS IN SPORTS[6]

Deepak Chopra in *Quantum Healing* also writes about boundaries. He says that individuals create their own illusions of not succeeding and negative beliefs, and these illusions and beliefs have boundaries. These boundaries prevent athletes or anyone from achieving their goals. Athletes can be in great shape and physically fit, but if they are not mentally prepared, have negative or limiting beliefs, they may not succeed to their fullest potential. Not believing that they can do it or don't deserve it or that it won't be good for them or safe for them will prevent them from achieving their goals.

Dr. Durlacker, *Freedom From Fear Forever*, believes that many athletes and teams suffer from slumps. They eventually pull themselves out of this created behavior but if treated could do it much sooner. Many times people are too proud or macho to recognize a fear that prevents them from achieving. In golf, it could be a fear of winning or losing, or a fear that the putt will go in the hole or lip the cup. It could be a fear of hooking or slicing, or a fear of a water hazard or out of bounds, *etc.* Obviously, fear can inhibit performance. Fearful people do not have the clear mental images that are important for success.

I won't go into the specifics of how to do the simple procedures to rid athletes of fears, but any coach, teacher or parent can learn easily by reading Dr. Durlacker's book.

---

[6] Adapted from *Freedom From Fear Forever* by James Durlacker.

COMMUNICATION

Good coaches, teachers, and parents as well, learn effective ways to communicate and then observe the responses they get. If those responses align with the goals you and your athletes have set, and values you both believe, then you have been successfully communicating.

What you say can influence people in a positive or negative way. Resistance from your athletes is a statement about how you are communicating. How you say something is much more important than what you say. Body language and the tone you use when speaking to someone are vital. How do coaches and teachers learn to communicate effectively? To begin with, they understand that their students make the best possible choices with the information they have, and that behind every behavior is a positive intention.[7] They also understand that communicating too much information at any one time can be a cause for confusion.

In any lesson, for example, you first develop **rapport** (a link, relationship, or understanding), which is an easy task once you do it a few times. Rapport is the ability to get into someone else's world, creating a bond. Creating a bond promotes trust, and then learning can take place easily. Once you bridge the gap between you and your students or athlete, coaching and teaching becomes a breeze. People like people who are like themselves, therefore imitating their body language, in a subtle way, is one way to develop rapport. **Pacing** and **leading** are the next steps. Pacing is the ability to change your attitude or behavior and be adaptable enough to respond to what you see and hear from someone else. Leading takes place when your atti-

---

[7] Chuck Hogan.

tude or behavior becomes a model for someone else to follow. The last step is closing. Always leave a student with a **positive** result. Rapport, pacing, leading and closing are effective ways to communicate and create a positive and powerful outcome. More success is possible when you focus on the outcome (this is what happened) and ways to affect it rather than concentrating on what is wrong.

Furthermore, to be good communicators, coaches and teachers need to learn more about themselves and the people they work with. When people are learning or thinking, they use their dominant learning sense. This sense, auditory, visual or kinesthetic is developed about the age of eleven or twelve. People learn in their dominant sense faster and easier. The coach or teacher needs to get out of their personal learning dominance and into the student's. Using language and words that facilitate this is essential. With a visually dominant learner, for example, the student will comprehend better when the coach uses words like *see, look*, and *picture.*

Generally, you can recognize someone's dominant sense by listening to the words they use. For example, **See** you later (visual), **Talk** to you later (auditory), or I'll get in **touch** (kinesthetic). Listen and you will quickly discover a student's learning dominance. More about dominant sense can be obtained by reading books on NLP.

Good communicators also need to know if their students or athletes are right brained or left brained and how they sort information. It is also helpful to know their personality type. Please see specific information on these topics later in this chapter. However, let me point out, **these labels are not important for the student to know.**

Something to Think About

A coach always has an open office so that athletes can come to talk without fear. The unconditional acceptance along with rules that are clear, concise and fair will make the coach's office a safe place for them to express their feelings and concerns. This is as important as a parent-child relationship.

Something to Think About

As long as you entertain the notion that there is something or someone else out there "doing it" to you, you disempower yourself to do anything about it. Only when you say, "I did this" can you find the power to change it. It is much easier to change what *you* are doing than to change what *another* is doing. The first step in changing anything is to know and accept that you have chosen it to be what it is. In the largest sense, all the "bad" things that happen are of your choosing. The mistake is not in choosing them, but in calling them bad. For in calling them bad you call yourself bad, since you created them.

You do not create the world's natural calamities and disasters, its tornadoes and hurricanes, its volcanoes and floods, or its physical turmoil, specifically. What you create is the degree to which these events touch you.[8]

---

[8] From the book *Conversations with God.*

RESPONSIBILITY

It is important here to say something about responsibility. Coaches, teachers and parents must accept responsibility for their actions just as much as students and children must. You are responsible for the choices you make as well as the results they produce. No one else is to blame. This understanding is foreign to some people, and must clearly be reckoned with at the first onset.

Not accepting responsibility usually rears its ugly head when we use it as a defense mechanism for things that don't work in our lives. We have a blind spot to the alternatives or choices that are available to us.

You may have heard golfers say:

"No matter what I do I can't seem to putt today."

"My game is bad because the people ahead of us are so slow."

"I just had a lesson and now my game has gone to pot."

"I'm late to practice because there was so much traffic."

In each case, there were other choices. We choose to be victims rather than take responsibility. This type of behavior is a learned behavior most likely learned in childhood. Sometimes it is a result of wanting to be right about the choices you have made and not wanting to be wrong.

Teachers, coaches and parents must take the responsibility of challenging their charges to recognize other possibilities available to them. It is a difficult task at times, but this kind of training will benefit them their entire lives.

Challenge their thinking with questions like the following:

How could you think about it in a different way?

Is there an alternative to your problem?

Is there any another way to go?

Can you think of another way to do it?
Pretend there is another choice. What could that be?
Take a guess at one or two other choices.
What would happen if . . . ?

COACHING POINTERS

Coaching an individual or team requires some considerations for success. We will look at some of these pointers throughout the book.

1. If you are not their swing coach, help them find a professional. This teacher should be someone you can work with as well as the student. He/she should be a person who will find out about the athlete and how they learn. He/she should be one who *loves to teach*. Athletes should resist bouncing from swing teacher to swing teacher looking for the magic and causing confusion. They should find someone they like and stick with them until that person cannot take them any further.

2. Instruct athletes to resist reading golf magazines and listening to television commentators for the tip of the week. This behavior can destroy their golf and confidence, because it is inevitable that they will think about what they read or heard on the practice tee or golf course.

3. Emphasize the short game. Athletes should practice their short game 75% of their practice time since the short game is 63% of their score. This includes putting which is 40% of their score.

4. Emphasize pitching. Good players pitch to within 6 feet of the hole. It can save at least 5 shots a round.

5. Be sure athletes know the distance they hit each club. Practice hitting balls in ten-yard increments. A football field works great. Have them hit ten balls with each club. Then take the nucleus of the shots. Keep a record of how far they hit balls with each club.

6. It is so important that each golfer gets fit for clubs. The lie, shaft and loft needs to reward each golfer's swing. It is a mistake to get clubs that do not fit. Hand-me-downs are usually the worst. The

clubs must fit the swing instead of fitting the swing to the clubs. All clubs in the bag need to have similar specifications so that golfers can swing the same with each club. One would never think of hitting tennis balls with loose strings in the racket or ski on skis with dull edges, or shoot pool with a bent cue. So why would anyone have clubs that do not fit their swing? I know that Henry Griffith Club Fitters do a great job. One especially comes to mind in Los Angeles is Ken Kenada at Industry Hills Golf Course. (See chapter VI on club fitting.) He is one of the best in the country.

7. Assist your golfing athletes in developing a constant and effective pre-shot routine.
8. Assist them in the aiming process.
9. Assist them in developing goals.
10. Permission is a belief more important than one might expect. Believing in yourself and believing that you are capable of success is critical.
11. Teach them how and what to practice (Chapter V) and about the discipline it takes.
12. Teach them when enough is enough. That there is time to stop tweaking their swings and accept the fact that their swing is good enough to play great golf, This doesn't mean to stop lessons forever.
13. Teach them that you can't always be perfect. "Golf is Not a Game of Perfect" so says Bob Rotella.
14. Teach them to play target golf with imagination and stop mixing targeting and mechanics.
15. Teach them to make good yardage books.
16. Teach them good course management.
17. Teach them to be honest, polite and kind to their playing partners.
18. Teach them to act, walk and talk like winners and do what winners do.
19. Teach them to take advice graciously without being threatened.
20. Teach them the purpose of anchoring and how to build a library of good shots in their brains.
21. Teach them good nutrition and why it is important.
22. Teach them how and why to condition their bodies.
23. Teach them how to develop good habits so they get what they want.

24. Teach them that there is no such thing as failure, only an opportunity to do something else.
25. Teach them to smile, have fun, win with grace and lose with dignity.

Emphasizing these points will assist in less stress and better results.

SUCCESSFUL COACHING

If you want to be successful, hang around with successful people (coaches).

It is easy to be successful if you hang around those who have had success. Successful people are willing to share their ideas because they are confident and have the ability to look at the bigger picture. They know that by sharing, the whole process gets better. And that, by the way, is how we learn, why we write books and give speeches. What you learn from reading this book, the author has learned from someone else and they have learned from others. That's how it works.

Someone is always ready to give the struggling teacher or coach some helpful ideas. So seek them out, call them on the telephone or write to them. Go to your library or bookstore and read what they say. Listen to everybody you can. Learn from every source available. Then use your imagination and create.

As a golf coach for many years, when I listened to people talk or give seminars or clinics, my imagination ran rampant. I remember once listening to Chuck Hogan speak at a seminar. "He said, celebrate your achievements. Get excited over them. Rub them all over you." At the next tournament, after a so-so round of golf by my team, they seemed to be complaining about their rounds. So, in the van on the way back to the hotel, I slammed on the brakes and pulled over to the side of the road. I asked everybody to think of a good shot that they had made that day. "Got one?" I asked. "Yes," was the reply. "OK, everybody out of the van. Ready? Think of that great shot you made today and jump up and down, yell and celebrate." They did just that. The atmosphere in the van change dramatically the rest of the night.

The coach provides an environment of unconditional acceptance. Sets the rules and parameters of behavior, which are absolutely precise and consistent. S/he admonishes breaches of behavior and points out appropriate alternatives while maintaining respect and acceptance of the child/student. Understands that there is a positive intent behind every behavior. Leads by example. The coach is the model and behaves consistent to what s/he expects from the student. Keeps the teaching of techniques and mechanics precise and short-term. Appreciates and nurtures the infinite potentials of the brain. Communicates that the winning is in the participation and playing of the game. Within that mentality, the coach does everything possible to ensure that all of the participants are winning. Makes the game a game, filled with fascination. Makes the playing environment a "safe place", free from ambiguity. Turns competition into cooperation.[9]

---

[9] "The Coach" by Chuck Hogan.

ADVICE TO COACHES

1. Become less reactive and more responsive. When we are reactive, we become annoyed, bothered and frustrated. Our decision-making is much more difficult and we often make decisions we wish we could change. Many times, we are rigid and stubborn.

2. When we are responsive, we are calmer. We hopefully see the bigger picture and take things less personally.

3. When we are adaptable, we usually make decisions that are more sensible. Opportunities are recognized and our minds are open. Success is the result.

4. Do what you do best and let others do what they do best. You coach and let others do the filing.

5. Do not be afraid to experiment. Risking is an important factor and results will guide your future.

6. The less you struggle with problems, the quicker they will be solved. Remember what you resist persists. I cannot tell you how important this is. There are people, for example who keep a grudge for months and even many years. Why do people hold grudges? Because people get something out of keeping grudges. They get to be right, angry, a martyr, *etc.* What a waste of energy.

7. There is always a solution. There is a way to get to where you want to go.

8. If things seem hard and you are a bit afraid, do it anyway.

9. Get out of your own way. Sit back, clear your mind, think back and listen to your inner self.

10. Become aware of your fears. Successful people know how to handle their fears.

11. Surround yourself with experts. People are always willing to share.

12. Do what you love to do. This is so important in our lives. Many people do not enjoy their jobs. They hate to go to work. They hate to get up in the morning to face another day. There are not many people who are good at what they do if they have that attitude.

13. Say thank you to those who help you. Get in the habit of writing thank you notes.

14. For heaven sakes, keep your sense of humor. Smile at your mistakes. Do not take yourself too seriously. Look at the positive side to find solutions. Ask for what you want from "I want a raise" to "I want this ball to go in the hole." You most likely will never get what you want until you ask.

PARADOXICAL COMMANDMENTS OF LEADERSHIP[10]

1. People are illogical, unreasonable, and self-centered.
   Love them anyway.

2. If you do well, people may accuse you of selfish ulterior motives.
   Do well anyway.

3. If you are successful, you may win false friends and true enemies.
   Succeed anyway.

4. The good you do today may be forgotten tomorrow.
   Do well anyway.

5. Honesty and frankness may make you vulnerable.
   Be honest and frank anyway.

6. The smallest men with the smallest minds can shoot down the biggest men with biggest ideas.
   Think big anyway.

7. People favor underdogs but may follow only top dogs.
   Fight for a few underdogs anyway.

8. What you spend years building may be destroyed overnight.
   Build anyway.

9. People really need help, but may attack you if you help them.
   Help them anyway.

10. Give the world the best you have and you may get kicked in the teeth.
    Give the world the best you have anyway.

---

[10] "The Edge"

TEN WAYS TO KEEP YOUR SANITY

1. Surrender. Make it easy by accepting what is and what is not, and then go for your goals.
2. Pretend for 60 days that you are not screwed up.
3. Get off your approval needs. The more you stay off them, the more frequently and generously you will be rewarded with positive feedback from yourself and others.
4. Stick your neck out there on the line and risk, then bask in the joy of the results that will inevitably come your way.
5. Keep your eyes and ears open. Opportunities are abundant, and you will create more by your willingness to be aware of and take advantage of what is going on around you.
6. Commit for all you can handle, and then handle whatever you have committed to.
7. Be honest with yourself and others. Keep your agreements. Trust that you have the ability to do whatever you want.
8. Reach out when you are distressed. Most people care about you and want to help you succeed.
9. Do something nice for yourself at least once a week.
10. Remember the universe rewards actions, not words.

Share your experiences.

WHAT TO DO AT THE BEGINNING OF THE SEASON

What you need to know about each individual.

At the beginning of the season coaches need to find out as much as possible about the students they are going to coach. So let's pretend that they are all new. You have never coached them before.

You need to discover the special attributes of each person so that you can have better insight into each individual and how he or she learns best. Everybody is special and learns in different ways. The following is what you need to know. Often it is best to learn about a student over a cup of coffee or Coke along with the tests and forms suggested below.

1. What are their personality styles? There is a simple and quick test to discover personality style at the end of this chapter. It only takes a few minutes. It's not perfect, but will give you an idea.
2. Find out if they are right- or left-brained so you know if they learn by looking at the whole picture first (right-brained individuals), or if they learn better by steps leading to the whole picture (left-brained individuals). See a quick test at the end of this chapter.
3. What kind of sorters are they? Do they always agree with you? Do they agree with you then offer a different view? Do they first offer a different view and then agree with you? Do they disagree with you right off the bat? There isn't a way of testing this that I know of, but just observing their responses will give you a clue. Then if you know this about an individual you won't be annoyed or distracted by their responses. There is no right or wrong here, only the way their brains sort information.

45

4. In what sense do they learn best? Visual, Auditory, or Kinesthetic? Even though we learn in all three of these senses, we seem to learn best in our dominant sense. You can discover this by using the simple test at the end of this chapter. Then you will be able to assist individuals with pictures and visual words, or rhythm and timing and auditory words, or by touching and feeling type words. People who are taught in other than their dominant sense generally have more difficulties learning.

5. Have they been fit for their clubs? After developing a reasonable skill level, it is most important that they be fit. They are many club fitters but few who do it in a rewarding way. The Henry Griffiths Club fitting system, in my opinion, is the best because they hit real balls off a lie board, which can be watched by a fitter and photographed by a computer or camera. It is important that student get fit for clubs so that their clubs reward their swing instead of fitting their swings to the club. Often you will find that students change their swings and compensate for non-fitting clubs.

6. How do they evaluate their mechanical skills and software skills? At the end of this chapter are forms you can use.

7. If they are in school, you need to know their schedule so that you can develop practice times.

8. What is the state of their physical fitness? Please see chapter on Physical Fitness and Nutrition.

9. You absolutely need to know what they want as far as their golf is concerned.

10. And finally you need to know what their goals are, who is going to assist them along the way, and who their supporters are.

On the following pages, you will find several forms that will help you to discover more about your children and/or athletes. Copy them and use them to make coaching and teaching easier and to facilitate the learning process.

PERSONALITY

The abbreviated personality test that follows will give you insight into how your students or athletes run their lives. There is no right or wrong here. They cannot pass or fail. It is a way to discover behavioral patterns, or a way of thinking, feeling and acting. It is a way for you and your students to discover more about yourselves. The most effective people are those who know themselves.

YOUR *PACE* PALETTE SCORE CARD

In the first horizontal row of four blocks decide which of the sets of three words seems to be *most* like you - and give that block a score of 4. Put a 4 in the circle in that block.

The group of words in that same row that seems *next most* descriptive of you will rate a score of 3, another group will get a 2 and the group which seems the *least* like you should be given a score of 1.

Then go on to the second horizontal row and score those blocks in the same way: 4 for the group that's most like you - 1 for the group that's least and 2 and 3 for the ones in between.

1st Row	Spontaneous Impulsive Impetuous ◯	Orderly Procedural Likes structure ◯	Authentic Outgoing Caring ◯	Philosophical Rational Competent ◯
2nd Row	Adventurous Active Daring ◯	Conservative Stable Planner ◯	Vivacious Communicative Cooperative ◯	Determined Curious Inventive ◯
3rd Row	Skillful Love excitement Optimistic ◯	Parental Dutiful Teacher ◯	Dramatic Self-actualizing Persuasive ◯	Ingenious Perfectionist Searcher ◯
4th Row	Jokester Light-hearted Witty ◯	Makes the rules Dependable Traditionalist ◯	Idealist Supportive Harmonious ◯	Loner Complex Composed ◯
5th Row	Open minded Bold Explorer ◯	Strong opinions Reliable Steadfast ◯	Empathic Romantic Compassionate ◯	Theoretical Intellectual Individualist ◯

Now add the numbers in each of the vertical columns and put the total in these squares.

☐	☐	☐	☐
RED	**YELLOW**	**BLUE**	**GREEN**

© 1992 - The *PACE* Organization

48

Personality and behavior strategies:

Red:
Demanding
Director
Dominating
Impatient
People mover
Resists personal criticism

Power and authority
Freedom from restraints
Results
High fives
Bet

Blue:
Interactor
Intimating
Recognition seeker
Disorganized
Fearful of social disapproval
Resists personal rejection
Impulsive

Inclusion with others
Enjoyment and friendliness
Prestige
Recognition
Fun
Share

Yellow:
Stabilizer
Servicing
Worker
Possessive
Fearful of risk taking
Resists sudden, vague changes, loss of security
Safety seeking

Appreciation and sincerity
Cooperation and sincerity
Predictability and personal
Productivity

Green:
Calculator
Conscientious
Cautious
Reserved precisionist
Overly critical
Fearful of imperfection
Resists criticism of their ideas or work

Work autonomy
Freedom from personalization
Professional development
Open ended
Low risk direction
Realistic, effective trade-offs

Red
Dominate, Adventure

I like being free to do things my own way.

Where are the new frontiers? I want to explore.

Life is a wonderful game—let's play.

Where's the action for the problem, let me at 'em!

Variety and excitement are fun and stimulating.

Give me a challenge—I'll handle it now!

I love the spotlight—watch me perform.

Let's find a new and different way to do it.

Freedom is important, don't fence me in.

Rules that don't make sense can be broken.

Bells are for ringing, mountains for climbing.

Reds tend to be more concerned about what's happening right now than in the future.

Adventurous hobbies, impulsive behavior, if it isn't fun—forget it.

Easy to ignore clutter. Generous, sharing, helpful. Waiting is awful. They love fine tools, instruments and the artist's brush. Easily bored and restless. Reds learn by doing, experiencing. Naturally **competitive**, witty and charming. Defeats are temporary. Exciting, light-hearted and joyful.

Yellow
Systematic, Responsibility

I value rules, tradition and authority.

I have a clear idea of what people should do.

I want to belong.

I handle details well and I'm a hard worker.

I am useful, productive, a contributor.

I like to care for others—look out for them.

I want to anticipate and prepare for the future.

The home and family is the core of society.

It's important to have rules, laws and controls.

I appreciate awards and public recognition.

I provide stability within an organization.

I demonstrate my love in practical ways.

Yellows are loyal, dependable, punctual, trustworthy, and they know that everyone else should be too. Structure and order are very important. They establish and maintain institutions. Very reliable—the backbone of a stable social system. Yellows resist change and see hierarchy as essential to society, the company, and the family. Any leadership or authority role must be earned. They have strong urges to conserve, plan and perpetuate.[11]

---

[11] 1992 - The Pace Organization

Blue
Interactive-Harmony

Relationships are important to me.

I want to have lots of friends—share and care.

I have integrity, I'm authentic and unique.

I like helping others become what they can be.

People are lots more important than things.

I enjoy flowers, music, and romantic movies.

I love to help friends solve their problems.

My hunches work, I'm very intuitive.

Empathy and sympathy are both easy for me.

I thrive on recognition and acceptance.

I'm really good at motivating people.

Blues see the possibilities in others and in themselves. Striving for authenticity, they want to become what they can be. Uniqueness is important, yet they can shift identities to fit the situation. Life is a search for meaning. Warmth and compassion flow easily and with sincerity. Devoted friends, they love to talk, share and help. Blues are imaginative, very creative and have lots of sensitivity to the thoughts and feelings of other people.

Green
Systematic-Curiosity

Searching, learning, understanding is fun.

I love puzzles, problems and finding solutions.

I like to work independently.

Intelligence, justice and fairness are important.

I want to be correct—to do things right.

It would be great fun to explore the universe.

Once I've found the solution, others can take over and put it into action.

My calm exterior may hide some inner turmoil.

I love to create a brand-new idea.

Being competent is absolutely essential.

I want my brain to manage my emotions.

Greens want to know all there is to know about everything. They like to analyze, probe, study, invent, investigate and explore. Non-conforming and independent, they tend to appear calm, cool and collected most of the time. The worst situation for a Green would be to appear stupid. If there's a time to read, outside of important books and journals, mysteries or science fiction will be the logical choice. They love abstraction and puzzles.

Right Brain-Left Brain

Answer these questions. Pick the one that is most like you not the one you would like to be. Be honest. This is not a test and you cannot be wrong.

___I prefer to write in print	or	___in cursive script
___I prefer non-fiction	or	___fiction
___I prefer doing arithmetic	or	___work
___I do things one-step at a time	or	___in random order
___I always wear a watch	or	___ask others for the time
___I prepare for performance	or	___dive in and see what happens
___I am on time for all appointments	or	___occasionally late
___My work requires detailed awareness	or	___a view of the entire project
___I learn by listening	or	___strictly by doing
___I learn through repetition	or	___by grasping the idea
___I learn by seeing	or	___by doing
___I ask "how"	or	___just "do"
___I balance my checkbook	or	___wait for the bank statement
___I fold socks and underwear	or	___pile them in the drawer
___I read instructions carefully	or	___just dive in
___I add up the parts to get the whole	or	___see the whole and then the parts
___I hear the words	or	___the melody of the song
___Mistakes are bad	or	___will get over it
___Do I need lessons	or	___just go play golf
___There is a right way to swing	or	___getting the ball to the target is it
___I am aware of myself	or	___the desired golf shot

___I go slow	or	___I go fast
___I review the test paper	or	___finish and turn it in
___I reread notes and letters	or	___finish and send them
___I take careful notes	or	___listen to the teacher
___I do the drills in task preparation	or	___just do the activity
___Rules are made to be followed	or	___to be followed by others
___If it makes sense I'll do it	or	___I'll do it to see if it makes sense
___I squeeze toothpaste from the bottom	or	___I just squeeze
___I warm the car engine	or	___I start the car and take off
___My clothes closet is arranged	or	___shirts and pants randomly hung
___My desk is orderly	or	___a comfortable mess
___My car gets very regular service	or	___kind of regular service
___I have written goals	or	___just know what I want
___I know what right is	or	___different strokes for different folks
___The world consists of waves and particles	or	___waves, particles, both and more
___I read the front page	or	___comics and sports page
___Clothes make the person	or	___if it feels good, wear it
___$E=MC^2$	or	___I sit on the rainbow in 2 places simultaneously
___Mankind will never levitate	or	___it is just a matter of time

_____   **TOTAL** _____

Add up the checks on left and right. Are you predominantly left or right in your view?

Left Brain Learners

Learn quickly when presented **with DETAILS**, which are given **VERBALLY** in a **SEQUENCE** with **REAL** and **LOGICAL** terms.

Learning aids such as whiffle balls and swing drills are useful.

Left-brain students are ideal learners of pre-swing and swing mechanics. They tend to be disciplined, and work hard on drills and practice routines. They tend to ask questions regarding the details and technical approach to any portion of the game. Their improvement as a player tends to be slow but steady until they have exhausted the basics of technique, at which time they will become a victim of 'paralysis by analysis' by digitizing (changing the flow of the swing from a continuous motion to a stop start motion) each part of the swing. They need to graduate into pure target golf, utilizing target imagery and intuitive shot making skills. Their most limiting inclination will be the reliance on analysis of technique and self-awareness.

Right Brain Learners

Learn quickly when presented with the **WHOLE** idea or the big picture. For example, they need to **SEE** and **FEEL** the entire swing rather than the details. They can picture **NON-VERBAL** instruction and **INTUITIVELY** understand how things work. They are **NON-TEMPORAL** unaware of time constraints. They learn **RANDOMLY** rather than sequentially and are analog (whole, continuous) rather than digital (pieces) oriented. They prefer to actually hit balls and be on the course, experiencing golf **CONCRETELY** rather than do drills. Their results are often described in terms of **FANTASY** instead of the objective reality of the left-brain learner. They tend to improve very quickly at scoring and creativity, but may later be restricted in improvement due to the lack of forming habits early in their development.

FUNCTION OF THE RIGHT AND LEFT BRAIN

The right and left brain perform different functions. Coaches and teachers need to understand how the brain works so that instruction can take place with ease. If the teacher knows which brain hemisphere is dominant in a student, he/she can better understand their thinking.

Briefly, it is the left brain that does the analyzing and learning the mechanics of a skill. The right brain is responsible for playing the game on the golf course, or should be. When golfers play the game and emphasize ball to target, great play can take place.

Any analytical thinking or mechanical emphasis, which is a left-brain activity, on the golf course is counter-productive. Left-brain activity or learning skills should be done on the range or in a room without a ball. This is a difficult concept for people to comprehend. because golf has always been taught on the driving range with a ball and still is. What is not understood is that the brain is not able to do both at the same time and therefore confusion takes place and learning is stalled.

It is important to mention here the cycle of competence that is best described by Chuck Hogan and illustrated at the end of this chapter. When a skill is taught, learned and practiced over a period of time, it becomes a habit. You never forget it. It is like riding a bicycle, tying your shoelaces or opening a door. You do these things without thinking about it. When you can do something without thinking, it is a habit. A habit can be good or bad. How many times have you heard, "I have this bad habit"? Well, you learned how to do it very well, and you are stuck with it until you learn a habit to replace it.

THE CYCLE OF COMPETENCE

How do we learn the skills in golf or the skills in any sport? Or how do we learn anything? How did you learn to tie your shoelaces? There is only one way the brain learns to do something and it doesn't matter if it is right or wrong, good or bad. The brain just learns. Here is the process very simply put.

You see it, feel it or hear it, and create a picture in your mind. How clear that picture is will determine how proficient you will be. You will know how clear the picture is when you can actually *do* what you have seen, felt or heard.

After you can "do the picture" you have formed in you mind and you **repeat** it many times you will create a habit. In the beginning, you will have to consciously think about it. You will know it is a habit when you can do it without thinking.

This is how learning takes place and habits are formed. A word of warning, however, is not to interfere with this process by allowing deviations to occur before the habit is formed. Confusion will take place and you will have to start over.

Teachers, coaches and learners must understand this process in order to make learning effective.

SENSORY DOMINANCE WORKSHEET

Which of the following best describes you?

Appearance

___ Dress neatly and brightly, orderly and pressed. Appearance oriented.
___ Moderate approach to fashion, dress for mobility.
___ Dress casually and comfortably.

Voice and Speech Pattern

___ Quick, high-pitched, to the point, animated, often in bursts.
___ Rhythmic, resonant, measured, with a definite cadence.
___ Slow, deep, oozing with occasional pauses.

Breathing

___ Rapid, shallow, high in the chest. Often short of breath when speaking.
___ Rhythmical, measured, from mid-chest.
___ Slow, deep, from the diaphragm.

Walk and Movement

___ Move briskly, efficiently and purposefully.
___ Move gracefully with a distinct cadence, bouncy.
___ Move slow and casual, very grounded.

Imagination

___ Vivid, rich in visual content, very detailed.
___ Flowing, more general, sounds and voices prevalent.
___ Lots of tactile feelings, very low on details, very intuitive.

Facial Gestures

___ Movement and changes around the eyes during pauses in speech; blinks, squints, eyebrows raise; eyes search up, left and right for answers.
___ Movement and changes around the ears and mouth during speech pauses, ahhs, umms; eyes search side, left and right for answers.
___ Movement and changes from the neck down primarily during pauses in speech; eyes search down and to the right for answers.

Reading

___ Would rather read than be read to; fast reader, likes to stop occasionally and visualize scene; strong successful area.

___ Moves lips and says words when reading; enjoys reading aloud and listening; often slow because of sub-vocalizing, likes passages of dialogue best.

___ Likes plot-oriented books, reflects action of story with body movement; likes action stories, points when reading.

Writing

___ Having it look OK is important, neatness important also.

___ Tends to talk better than writes, likes to talk while writing.

___ Thick, pressured handwriting; not particularly strong area.

Spelling

___ Good speller, can actually "see" the words; can spell in reverse.

___ Uses phonetic approach, sounds it out, rhythmically groups letters.

___ Counts out letters with body movements, writes out word for checking.

Learning in General

___ Learns best with overall view and purpose; needs details; cautious until mentally clear; memorizes by picture; has trouble remembering verbal instructions; organized, observant, quiet, deliberate; visual aids helpful.

___ Learns best by talking internally and externally; learns by listening; memorizes by steps; can repeat back and mimic pitch, tone and timbre of original information; spoken language easier than math and writing.

___ Learns best through manipulating and actually doing; responds to physical rewards; physically oriented; early large muscle development; memorizes by walking and seeing; responds physically.

Conversation

___ Interested in getting the whole picture, very detailed.

___ Loves discussions, has a tendency for tangents and telling the whole sequential event.

___ Not especially talkative, uses gestures and movements, touches people and stands close.

Expressing Anger

___ Get silent and seething.

___ One big outburst.

___ Storm off with clenched teeth and fists.

Attracted to People

___ Who have a unique or interesting appearance.
___ Who have a nurturing voice and a graceful manner.
___ Who have a warm, genuine appeal and a willingness to touch and hug.

Interests and Hobbies

___ Photography, flying, painting, reading, sketching, films.
___ Music, dancing, skiing, skating, speaking.
___ Sports, woodworking, gardening, massage.

Recall

___ Remembers what was seen.
___ Remembers what was said.
___ Remembers an overall impression of what was experienced.

Other

___ When bored looks around and doodles; can re-arrange information (ex: reciting telephone numbers in reverse); often rub neck when pondering; tend to believe in first impressions; tend to hunch shoulders; easily distracted by things they see; remember faces well.
___ When bored talks to themselves and hums; comfortable being alone; often gesture towards their ears; often use defocused gaze while thinking; whispering is a real attention grabber; remembers names well; interpret moods through tone of voice.
___ Fidget when inactive; above average athletic ability; are in touch with feelings; are distracted by movement; interpret moods through body language.

Results

Number of first choices_____ Visual Tendencies

Number of second choices_____ Auditory Tendencies

Number of third choices_____Kinesthetic Tendencies

TO BE MORE EFFECTIVE AT GOLF

Visuals

They can "see" how it is supposed to be done. They are able to lock on to a specific target. They process information quickly and are best when they are brisk and efficient. They need to see the target, be singular in their objective and stay on task. They learn best through the use of video, still frame photography and with the help of grid lines and props. They are fast learners and need to be presented information quickly or they become bored.

Auditories

They need precise instructions and literal directions. They need to maintain a sense of rhythm and motion throughout the processing and execution of their stroke. They learn sequentially and need to be provided with information beginning at the beginning and staying on track until the end. They do best with general targets and by achieving good balance. They feel their swing in their feet. Music and soothing nurturing voices are helpful.

Kinesthetics

They need to "feel" how it is supposed to be done. They need to be grounded and process their shot slowly until it feels correct. They perform best when they are able to indulge their sense of touch. They learn best through the use of drills and by holding key positions of the swing. They do best by going slowly and learning "one chunk at a time."

Questionnaire

Name:

Campus address:

Campus phone:

Cell phone:

Social Security Number:

School ID number:

Shoe size: Short size: Shirt size:

Glove size: Jacket size:

Clubs: Irons:

      Woods:

Have you ever been fit for clubs by a professional teacher/ club fitter?

What is your:
      Lie angle?   Grip size?

      Shaft?   Length?

      Loft?

      Face?

      Trajectory? High? Low? Standard?

      Degree in driver?

      Wedges?

      Putter?

Information Form for UCLA Golf Team Members

Name: Date:

Home Address: Home Phone:

Social Security Number:

School Address:

School Phone: Cell Phone:

Student ID Number:

Passport Number: Expiration Date:

Clothing Sizes (American sizes):

Shorts: Pants:

Rain Gear size: Inseam length:

Shoe size and width:

Shirt: Men's shirt size:

Visor: Baseball hat:

Glove size:

Height: Weight: Bust: Waist: Hips:

Equipment Information:

Irons:

Woods: Please check: Driver: 3 4 5 7 8 9 11 Driver loft: Brand:

Wedges:

Putter:

Golf ball: Compression:

Yardage: How far do you hit the following clubs?

Driver: 3:   4:   5:   7:   9:   11:

1   2   3   4   5   6   7   8   9

Wedges: Pitching: Gap or T: Sand:

GOLFER'S PROFICIENCY INDEX

RATE 1 TO 5 FOR EACH OF THE FOLLOWING:

1 = Dysfunctional for scoring efficiency.
2 = Intellectually accommodated but lacks integration into game and proficiency.
3 = Functionally O.K. but needs improvement.
4 = Fundamentally good, on again, off again in proficiency and consistency.
5 = Mastered and forgotten, consistently proficient, given tolerance for human error. Plenty good enough to be an efficient scorer.

Remember the best golfers in the world average 12.2 Greens hit, 9.6 fairways hit, and 30 putts per round, so do not compare yourself to perfect. Compare your present skills against the rating of the skills given to yourself if you were playing to your desired level.

____ Hold	____ Humor
____ Stance	____ Self-esteem
____ Swing	____ Self-nurturing
____ Balance	____ Imagination
____ Conserve/Expend	____ Concentration and attention
____ Balanced finish	____ Course management
____ Pitch	____ Practice efficiency
____ Chip	____ Beliefs
____ Sand	____ Routines
____ Specialty shots	____ Self-knowledge
____ Long putts (lag)	____ Preparation and rehearsal
____ Mid putts (6' to 24')	____ Mental practice
____ Short putts (6' to 1')	____ "Permission"
____ Driver (fairways hit)	____ Defined goals
____ Fairway woods	____ Goal setting skills
____ Long irons (1,2,3,4)	____ Validation procedure
____ Mid irons (5,6,7)	____ Sensory signal awareness
____ Short irons (8,9,PW)	____ Relaxation skills
____ Scoring proficiency	____ Time and energy management
____ Attitude	____ Diet and nutrition
____ Sub-total	____ Sub-total

____ Total (both columns)
____ (your score) = ____%
200

Name:_____   Date: _____

Chuck Hogan

GROUND RULES

- We will come from absolute integrity.
- We will be dedicated to teamwork.
- We will be helpful and respectful to each other.
- We will participate 100%.
- We will come from excellence.
- We will come from commitment and trust.
- We will take care of each other.
- We will support each other in achieving our goals.
- We follow the rules.
- We will cherish our University and represent our team with dignity at all times.

Commitment to Success Contract

1. I swear on my honor to commit to the following schedule that is attached to this contract.

2. I swear that I will practice my short game at least 65% of my practice time.

3. I will devote full attention and intention to every practice, and will not waste time.

4. When I play golf, I will give it 100%.

5. If I do the above, I will reap the benefits at the next tournament.

Signature_____

Date_____

REDEEMING TRAITS

Attitude, desire, patience, and persistence are a great combination that spell success in any man's language. These traits allow athletes/coaches/teachers to gain confidence, become more consistent and improve performance.

Great athletes do whatever it takes to keep themselves in shape and their game sharp. Great coaches do whatever it takes to see that this happens.

Players come and go. The ones who become successful, great talent or not, are the ones who have patience, superb discipline and a desire to be the best. And that goes for great coaches too.

Coaches can guide and assist athletes, but the athletes themselves are the ones who have to do the doing. Having a mentor is a sign of maturity. Being a mentor or coach or teacher involves great responsibilities. Mentoring takes the same dedication, commitment and patience as being a great athlete. There are many ways to "skin a cat." The first step is becoming aware; then it is up to you. This information is for people who want to get better at what they love to do. Having a passion for what you do is a great asset. It makes each day a new adventure. Wouldn't it be fun if you jumped out of bed every morning and yelled, "I get to coach today." Or "I get to play golf today." Maybe great coaches or athletes don't actually do that, unfortunately, but I'll guarantee that is the way they think.

Have you ever lain awake at night and dreamed of a way to do something different or a way to solve a problem? Great ideas are born that way, and people's imaginations find many ways to accomplish tasks.

Something to Think About

That's it, that's it. That's the way to do it!

Good coaches tend to become what they think of themselves just as athletes or anyone else as a matter of fact. Determination is the key and coaching is no exception. It takes hard work. It takes time. You learn by mistakes and taking risks. Confidence comes from repetition and believing in yourself.

And what is truly wonderful in coaching is that you have the opportunity to guide and direct people in making good choices and developing good habits. How fortunate you are!

HOW TO MAKE PARENTS YOUR PARTNERS

Coaching is rewarding. It is fun. It is challenging and it can be difficult at times. Being able to handle all the ramifications it presents is what it is all about. Having parents as partners is a big plus. Their support and cooperation is necessary for both athlete and coach.

1. Keep parents informed with telephone calls, e-mail, newsletter or visits.
2. Send them statistics.
3. Give them a copy of the rules.
4. Give them a schedule of tournaments.
5. Inform them where you will be saying at tournaments and give them phone numbers of hotel or the place you will be staying.
6. Inform them of the spectator rules at tournaments.
7. Get to know them.
8. Have a pre-season open house.
9. Be sincere.
10. Explain the program's philosophy.
11. Have a year-end banquet to give awards, honor athletes, and invite the parents.
12. Send pictures.
13. Be informative with problems, if you must consult them, and explain solutions or options.

When parents are included or at least informed, they will be more likely to assist and partner with you. However, remember blood is thicker than water. They will be the athlete's advocates, nine times out of ten, if push comes to shove.

RECRUITING AND THE COLLEGE EXPERIENCE

Playing on a college team in any sport is a valuable experience awarded to few. If the opportunity arises, student athletes have a chance to learn valuable skills that will take them through the rest of their lives, whether it be in professional sports, the corporate world or family life. Ideally they will have a coach who will take them to the highest performance level in their sport, be a great role model and care enough about them personally not to let them fail. A coach has a great responsibility not only to guide them in their endeavor to be a great athlete, but also to help mold their lives and prepare them for the future.

Recruiting is probably the single most important factor in having a successful team. What if you had a team composed of Olympic champions or a team of US Amateur champions. Do you think you might have a good team? Once you have the "horses" you can begin. A good recruiter can have a great team and be very successful. However, this does not necessarily mean that the recruiter is a good coach. There are different ability levels of teams as there are individuals. One school may go after the top blue ribbon athlete and another school may go after the next level or the ones with potential that the coach believes can be developed. The reasons for this are numerous. For example, the school may be situated in a place where there is always good weather. The school may have exceptional practice facilities. The school may have a winning tradition or be known as a great academic school. Each school is different both athletically and scholastically, Each coach is different. The later can be illustrated by the contrasting styles of John Wooden and Bobby Knight.

Student athletes should consider all facets of the schools they are considering including climate, location, size, coach, athletic program, academics, social, potential for future opportunities, *etc.*

Coaches use many factors to evaluate student athletes.

- Good student
- Good attitude on and off the golf course
- Athletic ability
- Physical competence
- Dress and composure
- Ability to fit in with the rest of the team
- Resume
- SAT scores
- Grade point average
- National experience in tournaments
- Competitive record
- Assessment of talent by the coach
- Videos
- Interviews with parents, counselors and high school coaches
- Letters of recommendation
- Opinions of the freshmen athletes already in the program who have competed with them in the past
- Opinions of other knowledgeable people.

The role of the recruiter is to recruit the best possible student athletes for their program. They may be the blue chipper or, in the opinion of the coach, someone who will step up to the task, a sleeper so to speak. The role of the athlete's family, her academic record and coachability are very important criteria.

The role of the family is extremely important to young athletes. College athletes are in the prime of life; they are maturing and leaving the nest to seek independence as well as still needing structure in their lives. The family is a big part of this process. How they are raised and supported throughout their collegiate experience will play a big role in their success as student athletes. The parents must be willing to take a supportive role and encourage them in their endeavors. They must continue to be role models. They must be prepared to let go and allow their sons/daughters to experience on their own. Student athletes must be allowed to achieve for their own reward and not be a slave to someone else's expectations. They must let the coaches do the coaching. Ideally they will have a good coach that will assist them in success, nurture them and not let them fall by the wayside.

A strong academic background will help the student compete at a top level. Most coaches believe that if they recruit athletes with good academic backgrounds, they will have less to worry about. If they are good students, they usually can manage their time, set goals, establish priorities and are able to handle the rigors of practice and time out of class to attend tournaments.

Coachability is always a plus. Student athletes must have open minds and be willing to listen and take advantage of their opportunities. Most coaches want what is best for their athletes. They should do whatever it takes to provide an environment where the athlete improves as a person and player.

RECRUITING SUCCESS

To be a good recruiter, you will need to have certain skills and be tuned into the important considerations of what works and doesn't work when enlisting someone in your life.

What you need to know.
1. Know the NCAA rules. Chapter 13 in the NCAA manual is the key.
2. Know all the information about your school including: academics, services and facilities.
3. Know all about athletic and academic scholarships.
4. Know where you can get information. Have a resource person at your school to help you get information.
5. Know how your competitors recruit.

How to proceed.
1. The first contact.
   The first time you meet a recruit is critical. You need to establish rapport immediately. (Read about rapport in the chapter on Neuro Linguistic Programming.) First impressions are an important key. Dress appropriately, have your guns in order and know what you are talking about. Be friendly and concerned about their future. It is very helpful to send a biography form to recruits when they are in the eleventh grade in order to obtain background information. This information allows you to be intelligent at your first meeting. Please see form at the end of this chapter.

2. <u>Determining the concerns of parents and student-athletes.</u>
   As soon as possible, find out what the parents want for their son or daughter and what is important to them This information will allow you to address those concerns and highlight them from your university's point of view.
3. <u>Finding out who will be making the decision.</u>
   Most often, the parents will say that it is the decision of the student-athlete. However usually someone is influencing that decision. You must know who that person is so that you can address their concerns.
4. <u>Listening to athletes and parents and reading between the lines.</u>
   Listening is the way you get information. Stop talking, listen and ask the right questions. You will be able to ask the right questions when you hear what they are saying. You can then sell them on your university.
5. <u>Have a plan for each recruitable athlete.</u>
   Plan ahead. Sometimes the early bird gets the worm.
6. <u>Plan home and school visits as soon as possible.</u>
   Reserve the date with the athlete. Be sure to send all the information necessary to recruit for school visits including travel arrangements where they will be staying, schedule of events and what they should bring. Make the school visit the best visit possible. Engage the whole team in the recruiting process during the recruit's visit, and gear the visit to the specific interests of the prospect. Be sure you enlist the student-athletes on your team in the planning process. If possible, get the parents to attend sometime during the official visit. You can arrange special plans for them while the recruit is with the team. It is a good sign when the parents are willing to participate in the school visit. Remember, if you recruit the parents, you will know what you are getting in the recruit.
7. <u>How to present your program.</u>
   Make a list of valuable assets your school has to offer, *i.e.* athletic and academic reputation, tutorial support, size of classes, social life, career guidance, internships, foreign student and minority programs, libraries, outstanding fields the university is known for, faculty, dorms, and churches. Compare them to other schools the athlete is considering. You might

make a tally sheet for comparison. Other items you might want to compare are: traditions, famous former athletes, quality of present team, schedule and travel opportunities, level of competition, alumni support, facilities, record of team, schedule, outstanding coaches, the relationship between the women's and men's teams, majors offered, and new student programs. Big school/small school might be a problem as well as location and climate. Furthermore, you might have to explain how scholarships are awarded, what a full scholarship consists of, and what a partial scholarship includes. Summer school, books, room and board, injuries, insurance, and fifth year financial coverage can also be concerns of the prospective student-athlete and their parents.

8. <u>The use of videos</u>.

It is helpful to show either a general university video or highlight tape of your program in the home visit since these are the only two tapes allowed by NCAA rules. A highlight video shows your players in your program and how they are doing, while a general university video provides them more information about the campus life and campus community. It is a good tool for breaking the ice and starting the home visit.

9. <u>Presenting your philosophy and program</u>.

Some written information here would be a good idea. It can be a great handout that you can go over with the athlete and parents. However, you don't need to discuss everything you know.

10. <u>Getting a commitment</u>.

There are several commitments necessary along the way. The home visit, the school visit, telephone commitment and the final big one, the letter of intent. The first two are self-explanatory. Telephone contacts on the other hand can be more difficult.

In every telephone call you make to the prospective student-athlete, get some kind of a commitment. It could be a return call, a paper to send, a form to fill out and send, an article about them from a newspaper, an e-mail or other information. You will know they are interested if you receive these small commitments. The letter-of-intent commitment is the hardest one. It is a major decision for both coach and recruit and sometimes can be very stressful. The sooner you ask for the commitment, the sooner you will know where your school fits into the equation. Asking the question brings up a great deal of emotions. Nobody likes rejection or wants to lose a desired relationship and nobody wants to take second place. When asking for a commitment, summarize how your program fits the needs of the prospect from the information he/she has related. Your personality will dictate how you ask. Be firm, be positive and be yourself. After the first commitment don't give up until you see the letter of intent with your own eyes.

11. Being honest and straight forward.
    Be truthful in your conversations. People can always tell when you are padding the information. Besides, it will come back to bite you.

12. Come from your heart.
    This is probably one of the most important choices you can make. Coming from your heart will assist you in every occupation or relationship.

13. A good recruiter has backups if the one you want turns you down. In these days of comparative shopping, it is important to set a deadline schedule with your top recruit in order not to lose your back up recruit. Set an agreed to timetable for making the college decision. If your top recruit can't make the decision by then, move onto your next recruit with a similar timetable. If that doesn't work, move to you next recruit that fits the similar qualifications to the first two. It is important to get backups, because even the best programs don't get everyone they want. It is also important to keep your team viable. Getting at least one good recruit each year perpetuates the team. It is not a good idea to leave blank years because, as they graduate, you can have a year or two that is not up to par.

14. Decide you love to recruit.

15. Send thank you notes.
    Thank you notes pay off immeasurable. Thank all the people who assisted you. Thank the recruits who didn't commit and the ones who did.

RECRUIT COLLEGE COMPARISON CHECK LIST
(RATINGS BASED ON 1--BEST, 2-2ND BEST, 3-3RD BEST)

	UCLA		
ACADEMICS			
Major area of interest			
Internship experience			
Summer job around sport			
Academic Services for S/A			
Class pre-enrollment			
Tutoring within major			
Graduate School for major			
Overall Graduate School			
Job market in chosen field			
Overall support for your sport			
ATHLETICS			
School's sport athlete success			
Coaching staff experience			
Cooperation among all coaches			
Professional/Olympic possibilities			
Success of athletes after college			
Campus Sport Recognition			
Campus support of all sports			
Success of other sports			
USA Team/Post-Season opportun.			
Connections of coaching staff			
Strength & Conditioning Prog.			
Overall Athletic Facilities			
Sports Medicine Knowledge			
On-campus medical facility			
National Media Coverage			
Local TV/Radio/Newspaper cov.			
National Name Recognition			
Media Training Program			
Future Contacts/Endorsements			

CAMPUS COMPARISON:

UCLA

SOCIAL

Campus sports atmosphere

On-campus residence halls

Surrounding campus community

Closeness to the beach

Overall weather

Diversity of student body

Friends on the teams

Opportunity for new experiences

School friends on ath. int. teams

Team travel opportunities

Apt. campus walking distance

Variety of activities in local area

Driving to other recreational areas

Year-round playing opportunties

Free tickets to campus sports events

INTANGIBLES

Best place for athletic future

Best place for post-college athletics

Best place for academic major

Best year-round living conditions

Best year-round training conditions

Best overall ath.-academic combo

Best faculty support of athletics

Best chance for immediate playing

Best transition from HS to college

Best overall support staff for sport

Athletic significance to university

NCAA

The NCAA is the governing body for all institutions involved in intercollegiate athletics at Division I, II, and III. levels of competition. Division II and III do not give athletics scholarships, only academic scholarships.

The NCAA has certain rules regarding recruiting. Every recruit and coach must follow these rules. They govern what a coach and a student athlete can and cannot do. Individuals become prospective student athletes beginning with their freshman year in high school. Many will begin receiving questionnaires then. They should start early in their junior year to investigate universities. Athletes need to talk to former athletes, write for brochures, visit campuses on their own, read books on the different universities and write to a variety of coaches. During their senior year of high school, they may visit up to five universities on an "official visit" and can have as many unofficial visits as they need. They can also have contact with coaches after July 1 following their junior year in high school. This contact can be written or through e-mail. During their senior year, they can talk once a week on the phone. It is very important that families and athletes being recruited understand the NCAA rules. Anyone can obtain information from his or her school counselors or the NCAA. There are pamphlets on recruiting and what can and cannot be done. A word of warning: the rules are complicated and sometimes difficult to understand, but they are the rules and they must be followed accurately. The consequences for not following the rules can be severe for the university and the prospective student-athlete.

NCAA CLEARINGHOUSE

The NCAA Clearinghouse is an organization controlled by the NCAA that monitors all prospective student-athlete's academic records. They have core course requirements that have to be met as well as a minimum SAT score. There are thirteen NCAA core course requirements in English, math, science, social science and electives. The Clearinghouse uses a sliding scale that every prospective student-athlete must meet if they want to compete at the Division I level. The higher the GPA, the lower the test scores can be and vice-versa. All prospective student-athletes need to fill out an application, send the required monies, test scores and transcripts to be evaluated. When this is done, and only then, can the student-athlete be cleared for competition. Student-athletes can obtain applications from their counselors at their high school or write and/or call the NCAA.

FOREIGN STUDENTS: GETTING THEM INTO SCHOOL:
or
"If there is a will there is a way."

An Example:
> Note: For Division I College Coaches The following are the rules for getting foreign students into a Division I University. You can use it as a guide.

1. They must take the **SAT I** test. ACT is largely unavailable to foreign students. Have results sent to the Athletic Dept. **Code for UCLA is 4837.**

2. They should take the **Tofel** test. This determines the English, Reading and Writing ability. Have results sent to the Athletic Dept.

3. It is possible to take the **SAT II** test here at University High School, phone number 310-478-9833. Call to find out the dates given. They must have a check or money order, no cash. It is about $53 or $56. The address -11800 Texas Ave. Santa Monica, (Go west on Wilshire to Barrington, turn left. The school is between Westgate and Santa Monica Blvd. Go to the Barrington side of the campus by parking lot.) Test starts at 7:30 AM. Doors close at 8:00 AM. If on standby you need to fill out application so you must be there at 7:15 AM.

4. SAT test scores can be rushed to UCLA and the Clearinghouse with a small fee. It can be done by Visa from any country by calling the clearinghouse phone number 319-337-1492. The number is also on the form. Student must register with the clearinghouse and send the proper documents and fees. The Clearinghouse must clear student before she/he can compete or receive athletic aid.

5. Send an **original** of the Matura, Maturita (different names in different countries) but it is the Graduation Certificate, to UCLA or brings it with them when they come.

6. Fill out **intent to register** form.

7. Fill out **confidential financial statement**. It must be endorsed by the bank in their country and guarantee enough money for emergencies. The amount necessary is $5,500 if on full scholarship.

8. Fill out **statement of amateurism**. (Available in compliance office.)

9. Fill out **application for admission** and return to Athletics with check or money order for $40.00, payable to UC Regents.

10. **Visa** must be obtained at the American consulate in their country. It must be a student visa. **If by chance or necessity because of time and it is a visitors visa, it must have a statement or stamp on the passport that says** it is to be changed to a student visa. (F-1) It is a big problem to change it here so do it right the first time. If it is a visitors visa, go to Jimmy White, International Student Office Lawyer, 310- 825-1681, so that he can go to immigration and change it. He must take their passport with him. Do not mail it, in order to change it, it takes 6 months. Any visa problems see Jimmy White.

11. Student can not get a scholarship ($) without a social security number, and can not get a social security number without a proper visa. To get a Social Security number, go to the Federal Bldg. On Wilshire and Sepulveda. The office is on the 10th floor. Student must take student visa and passport with them and fill out application as a student. SS# takes about 10 days with approval of application and comes in the mail. However, there is a number to call to get the number sooner over the phone. Only the student can do this.

12. Fees need to be paid by Friday prior to the first week of class. If for some reason student isn't cleared yet the student must pay their fees in order to stay in school. If for some reason, the student does not have enough money to pay for tuition and fees, they can get a loan at the International Student office on Circle Drive. If by some chance the ISO runs out of available cash, the ISO can arrange to have the fees deferred for three to four weeks.

13. She/he must be registered in **12 units** in order to practice.

14. Student's record must be in the registrar's system to get classes.

15. Student must open a checking account.

16. Student must bring with them from their country and original document of their grades. (Transcripts) Documents can be faxed from their country initially, however originals must eventually be presented.

17. Of course all this must be done in a timely fashion, the earlier the better, but it can be done quickly if you are willing to put a great deal of time and effort into it. Take it from someone who knows. Good luck.

(Written by Jackie Steinmann)

MEMBERSHIP VALUE
UCLA WOMEN'S GOLF TEAM-1999

No Scholarship (Financial Aid)	Per Year	Per 4 years

• Golf Team Benefits

	Per Year	Per 4 years
Playing top golf courses	10,000	
Range balls	1,000	
Golf bags, head covers, travel bags	350	
Golf shoes, tennis shoes	375	
Uniforms	1,200	
Weight room	250	
Trainers	100	
Tutors	1,000	
Travel	10,000	
Sports Psychologist	100	
Special clinics	260	
Coach and assistant	8,000	
Total	**$32,535.00**	**$130,140.00**

• 50% Scholarship

	Per Year	Per 4 years
Educational Fees	3,863.00	
Books	1,100.00	
Golf Team Benefits	32,535.00	
Total	**$40,498.00**	**$161,992.00**

• 100% Scholarship

	Per Year	Per 4 years
Tuition and Fees	3,863.00	
Books	500.00	
Room and Board	6,832.00	
Golf Team Benefits	32,535.00	
Total	**$43,730.00**	**$174,920.00**

If student is out of state, an additional 38,296.00 is added for the 4 years.

Total for full scholarship-Out of State for 4 years   **$251,512.00**

The fifth year is not included in this analysis. It is an addition.

• Plus a great Education

Something to Think About

Children learn easily by doing, watching and acting as if they know how.

CHAPTER III

Teaching

TEACHING CHILDREN

The world of children's golf has reached new dimensions. Tiger Woods certainly has attributed to this explosion. And yes it is a good thing. Almost three million kids are taking up golf and it's increasing daily. On many golf courses and ranges new facilities are being made available to children. New programs are being developed and professionals are taking much more interest. And of course they should, because that's the future and where the money is. Because of this surge the corporate world is jumping on the bandwagon with equipment and apparel for the same reasons. What kind of golfers are in our future? Are you as a coach/teacher/parent mindful of your influence? How can we guide our youth and athletes?

When children are pushed into sports too early, when parents insist that they take lessons when they are not ready for lessons, children will burn out or be miserable and will not learn easily, especially if they are not having fun or playing the game. If they don't have a good foundation experienced in the earlier stages of their life and are forced to live up to their parents' or teachers' expectations and intense pushing, problems will occur.

There is a belief that in order to be good you have to be pushed. You can push yourself toward **your** objective, but being pushed toward somebody else's objective or goal is not in the best interest of the child. Let the child do it because he or she wants to. Let the child play free of pressure and fear. Let the child learn by her own self-direction through play and refrain from always teaching them. Provide the opportunities for them to learn that are self-directed and self motivated. Children will build self-esteem naturally, grow at their own pace and learn through their own imagination.

From *The World of Play* from the International World of Play Conference (Edited by Jessica Carter Kimmel, Ph.D. and Mary Ruth Moore, Ph.D.)

There are two main factors that influence children, **PRESSURE OR LACK OF IT AND PLAY.**

1. The consequences of adult pressure on children's organized games, *e.g.*, sports, are well known. The behavior of many adults today is regretful, disappointing and irresponsible. All one has to do is watch a Little League baseball game, or watch some parent during or after a so-so round of golf by their junior player. Here is an article from the *Los Angeles Times* dated Wednesday, August 8, 2001:

Mom Beaten After Son Scores Winning Run

SALT LAKE CITY—The mother of a boy who scored the winning run in a baseball game was knocked unconscious by two angry parents from the losing team, police said Tuesday.

After her 15-year-old son's run in the youth league game, two women allegedly poked the woman with an umbrella, hit her with a baby stroller and punched her in the face. She was unconscious when police arrived and was treated at a hospital for cuts and bruises. *Etc., Etc.*

More and more such incidents happen all the time. Is this the way we want our children to act?

2. Furthermore, many modern children grow so accustomed to being entertained these days that they become social misfits, incapable of intelligent human interaction and creative work.

Play is supposed to be fun. Just ask a bunch of children. You have a choice; it is not planned. One is free to do what one wants, free to imagine and create, to construct something that can lead to a product or a job, and the realization that sometimes work can be play. The important factor here is to understand in general what play *is* in order to know what it is not. Judging from the range of activities that are being substituted for children's creative play these days, the typical American adult appears to have an extremely limited view of the nature and importance of play.

The substitution of entertainment, video malls, TV, paid entertainment areas, *etc.*, for creative play and quality interaction with parents in homes and communities is deeply implicated in the growing problems of our society. American children rank last among children of industrialized countries on tests of physical fitness. They are the most violent, use more drugs, engage in sex at earlier ages, and thanks to overdoses of sedentary television viewing and junk food, they are growing more obese and developing early symptoms of risk for later cardiovascular diseases.

Play is central, indispensable, for cognitive (perception-awareness), social, language and motor development and as well as emotional mastery. Play isn't just fun. Play is a vital activity that prepares children for adulthood. In play, unlike in direct instruction, the child is always behaving beyond his age or everyday behavior. So it is important that teachers understand the nature and importance of play and know how to inhance their creativeness. Much has been written on the subject of play and its awareness, but suffice it to say in this book that understanding play is important in the development of children. So when substitution for play occurs, pressure and stress are manifested and/or instruction takes place too early by unsuspecting teachers and parents, severe harm can be done. Stop doing it. Stop pressuring children to succeed for your reasons, your gratifications. Stop allowing your children to watch TV excessively. Disallow video games in and out of the video arcades. Instead, take children to parks, libraries, play grounds, museums, *etc.* They will learn to run their own brains instead of having their brains run by others.

A CHILD BONDED TO ANXIETY
CAN NOT HELP BECOMING ANXIOUS.

→

BURN **OUR**

←

OVER COACHED YOUNGSTERS, THE GAME CRAMMED "DOWN THEIR THROAT". PARENTS OR LITTLE LEAGUE COACHES WHO, THEMSELVES, ARE ANXIOUS.

MANNERS AND ETIQUETTE

Let me make a few statements about manners and etiquette. The *World Book Encyclopedia* dictionary describes manners as "polite ways of behaving, and etiquette as conventional rules for conduct or behavior." (pp. 1182 and 676) Being polite is about feeling comfortable with yourself and making other people feel comfortable. Manners are predicted by the environment you are in at the time. Manners and etiquette have deteriorated in our culture over the last many years, and there has been a lack of concern in many young people. This looseness can be reflected in their athletic endeavors, also.

The anything-goes mentality by our youth nowadays often turns people off or is embarrassing. The dress-down manner in the workplace or the campus is misinterpreted, and many people are confusing casual with sloppy. People seem to behave the way they dress. Handshakes, table manners, how and when to introduce yourself and others are important skills in our society, as are cleanliness and neatness. If your athletes have not learned manners, how to hold a fork and knife, or how to iron their clothes and dress neatly through parental guidance, then it is the coach's duty to supply that information. The athletes may not like it at the time, and may even be resentful and claim that it is not important, but they will thank you someday. For when they attend a dinner, a meeting, or a banquet with sponsors, business people or their boyfriends or girlfriends, they will feel comfortable knowing that their behavior will not be embarrassing.

You can call in experts to talk to the athletes. Sometimes young people will listen to experts more attentively, but it is valuable for the coach to also show them the proper behavior. You are the model.

Teaching them how to hold a fork or spoon, how to eat soup, where the eating utensils, glasses, the bread plate and napkin go and when and how to use whatever, and how to pass dishes at the table and eat bread are important. Haven't you ever gone to a banquet where someone has picked up the wrong napkin or used the wrong bread plate? It can throw off the whole table and make the situation very uncomfortable. Likewise, stumbling when introducing someone can also be very uncomfortable when you are not sure how or when to do it.

Teaching manners and etiquette may be difficult and uncomfortable. **Do it anyway**.

Some things you can teach when the situation is warranted are:

- How to introduce someone.
- Table setting and where to start with utensils.
- How to hold a fork and spoon and how to use a knife.
- How to pass food and plates.
- How to eat bread and soup.
- Using the butter knife.
- Where your napkin is and how to use it.
- What to do with utensils when finished eating.
- When to begin eating.
- How to chew with your mouth closed.
- How to serve and remove plates.
- How a gentleman treats a woman and how a lady treats a man.
- How and what to wear and when.
- When to remove your hat, *etc.*

Manners and etiquette are almost the same in every country. There are few exceptions. It is a responsibility of the teacher, coach or parent to address this kind of behavior and insist on its achievement.

Something to Think About

Undermine, minimize, or undervalue what you do and you will undervalue who you are. Courage is choice. It takes courage, for example to be rich, different or disciplined, and it is those people in this world who are the successful ones. BEING NORMAL IS THE BOOBIE PRIZE. THE EXCEPTIONAL ATHLETES ARE THOSE WHO ARE DIFFERENT.

Values

Values are established ideals of life, customs and ways of acting that people regard as desirable. Values can change, but for the most part, they are taught in early childhood.

Sometimes, however, it is necessary to make a point even to adults. Here is an example:

Compassion

Compassion: The feeling for another's sorrow or hardship that leads to help.

A lesson in compassion began one week when I had just about had it with my team. One night I lay awake wanting to solve the problem. Then an idea struck me. I will pretend. The next day I put on the show of my life becoming an actress, maybe not Taylor or Spacik, but good enough. In the team meeting that afternoon, I told them how hard I had worked to see that they succeeded. How long I had coached, and how hard I tried to make a difference in their lives. They had really hurt me the last few days and their behavior was completely unacceptable. I explained that I was so offended and disappointed that they could go to practice by themselves and maybe I would see them in a day or two or three. I went out the door, shut it and left them pondering their behavior and thoughts. As I walked down the hall to my office, I yelled "Yes", and pumped my fist. I think I finally got to them. One hour later, they all entered my office and apologized. "We are really sorry, Coach."

The next day their attitude improved considerably.

You can create many ways to illustrate a point. Living by the Golden Rule is not a bad idea. "Do unto others what you would have them do unto you."

HELPFUL TEACHING HINTS

1. Teach in chunks. The brain is incredible. It will learn anything. It is much easier to learn when the teacher breaks down the information and teaches a little bit at a time. Too much information can be confusing. Remember less is best.

2. Know all your athletes and how they learn best, auditorally, visually or kinesthetically. Know if they are left or right brained so that you can present information to them in a better way. (See Chapter II)

3. Make the playing and teaching environment a safe place. Explain the playing and practice arena and the proper behavior necessary. Explain what is expected so that they are not intimidated. Explain safety requirements. Explain the rules and etiquette so that they are not intimidated.

4. Make golf a game and make it fun. If they are having fun, they will learn.

5. On a practice area, play get the ball in the bucket, umbrella or in the circle. It works for all ages.

6. Show them how to play the game. You are the model—be a good one. Let them see the good stuff.

7. Teach them that losing is not failure but only an opportunity to do something different.

8. Teach them togetherness and they will learn that competition means working together and cooperation.

9. Teach them good manners and behavior on and off the golf course.

10. Let their instructor do the swing mechanics unless you are their swing teacher.

11. Give children group lessons. They will learn better and have more fun in a group of their peers.

12. Encourage them and appreciate their accomplishments however small.

13. Start them off with one child's club. Many companies make children's clubs. Resist cutting down one of your own old clubs. For a child it's like swinging an ax which is way too heavy and stiff. It will hinder rapid learning. Once they show interest, you can purchase a starter set of children's clubs that many manufactories make. There are trade in possibilities when the clubs get to short. Henry Griffiths custom clubs is one such company located in Idaho and there are other manufacturers.

TEACHING ATHLETES HOW TO BE GREAT PLAYERS

This is adapted from Chuck Hogan's "To Be A great Player"

1. Find out what the student/athletes want. What are their goals?
2. Ascertain if they have permission, if they believe they can accomplish their goals.
3. Do they love to play golf and enjoy themselves?
4. Do they know how to relax and be at ease?
5. Can they maintain their sense of humor?
6. Teach them to be great inside of 100 yards.
7. Teach them to practice the short game 75% of their practice time.
8. Teach them to fall in love with their target and be totally integrated with it.
9. They must know their swing and own their mechanics.
10. They must learn to use their imagination when hitting a shot.
11. They must understand that it is important to be balanced physically, psychologically, emotionally and spiritually.
12. Teach them that there is no such thing as failure.
13. They must learn to be adaptable to situations and conditions.
14. Teach them to be great at doing what they do. Mediocracy does not do it.
15. Be sure they have golf equipment that complements their swing and a putter that complements their visual system.

16. Teach them to keep statistics so that they know where to shift focus.

17. Make them understand that the above are all choices.

EFFECTIVE TEAM MEETINGS
OR INDIVIDUAL MEETINGS

Being a leader takes practice. Getting others to talk and leading them into meaningful discussions is priceless. The less you talk and the more others talk the better leader you are. They certainly seem to enjoy themselves more, and they discover what you want them to do on their own. They will respect your leadership more and they will be more likely to change their beliefs, attitudes and behavior. Instead of less control, you will have more control.

First and foremost, be prepared. Plan your meeting on paper and have all your supplies ready. On the next page is an example of a plan and following this list are some examples of creative exercises. Use your imagination and come up with interesting ways to communicate. Make the meeting fun with jokes, pictures, games or things to do. Coloring is an example. Something to color related to the subject of the day keeps people involved. They are still actively listening. A good idea is to draw pictures or take pictures from somewhere like a coloring book and encourage them to color during a team meeting. If you give them permission to color like a child, they will fight over the color of crayons in the middle of the table. Examples of things to color are throughout the book. Use them as you like or make up your own.

Here are a few suggestions for your meetings:

1. It may be hard, but get everyone to participate. Do not let any one person monopolize the discussion. Direct questions to the ones not joining in.

2. Always wait for a response. Be calm and confident.

3. When you like what is said, say so and give appreciation and recognition.

4. Ask open ended questions, questions that do not have a yes or no answer. For example: What is your opinion? What has been your experience? What are your thoughts on this subject? How do you feel about this?

5. Your function is to lead and direct but not to overpower. Empower the team or individual you are working with. Make them take the responsibility.

6. Listen attentively to all. This is so important. Listening is as art. The patience it takes to listen until someone is finished sometimes takes a great deal of control on your part. Do not interrupt unless you really really must. At least wait until the end of the thought or sentence.

7. Always use the names of the people you are talking to.

8. Be pleasant and friendly and interested by your tone of voice and expression. Look people in the eye when you talk to them.

9. Ask for or have ready some supporting evidence whenever possible. This helps make ideas more believable.

10. Remember you are the model, act accordingly. If you want them to listen, then you listen to them. If you want them to be respectful, then you be respectful to them, *etc.*

USE YOUR IMAGINATION, BE CREATIVE JUST AS YOU DO

IN YOUR GOLF GAME.

TEAM MEETING PLAN: DATE:

<u>Room set up:</u> Crayons, drawing, calendar for week, statistics from Golf Stat.

<u>Announcements, Activities, Lesson:</u>

❖ <u>Birthday Celebration.</u>

❖ <u>Goals for the month:</u>

Genie drawing. Color drawing. If you had three wishes! Write the three wishes at the bottom of your drawing. What three wishes would you wish for this team? Discussion and mutual decision. (See drawing on page 213.)

❖ Collect good/bad notebooks.

❖ Qualifying rounds announcement.

❖ Discussion of Golf Stat statistics. Where do we need to work more efficiently individually and as a team?

❖ Write a short paragraph about your performance that might appear in the newspaper after the tournament is finished **next week**. How did you play and what was it like and how did the team do? Would anyone like to read their article? Tape this article to the mirror in your bathroom so that you see it everyday until the tournament.

❖ One-hour competition on the field pitching to buckets. Prizes to the winners.

<u>Notice:</u>
Pick up information about tournament on Tuesday in my office.
Practice at Wilshire CC at 7:00 a.m. tomorrow.

TEAM MEETING POINTERS

1. Be prepared, organized with a written plan.
2. Make it fun.
3. Invite participation.
4. Teach in chunks. (Too much information can be confusing.)
5. Do some physical activities.
6. Demonstrate when you can.
7. Give examples.
8. Have written handouts.
9. Make playing notebooks a must. (Good - Bad notebooks.)
10. Use stats to guide.
11. Be original. Use your imagination. Be creative. Use coloring.
12. Break into groups.
13. Use a chalkboard. Write an agenda on the board.
14. Get feedback. Ask questions.
15. Save all your lessons.
16. Have recognition time.
17. Hand out schedule for the week.
18. Make announcements or assignments.
19. Use the buddy system.
20. Evaluate.

EXAMPLES

INFORMATION FOR REGIONALS
MAY 6TH, 1998

Uniform for plane is warm-ups with white shirt
We are staying at Holiday Inn in Palo Alto (650) 328-2800

TUES.5TH   11:00 A.M.   Leave for Stanford. Meet at United. LAX-
United Shuttle. Eat something before you
come to airport. We will be eating dinner
in San Francisco!!!!

WED. 6TH   12:45 p.m.   PRACTICE ROUND
Tail plaid w/vanilla tail shirt. Blue hat w/ bl/wh
socks; blue belt

THURS. 7TH 8:00 Am.   1ST ROUND- Hole #10
Beige shorts w/ white new tail shirt w/ blue&yellow
lettering white hat

FRI. 8TH   2ND ROUND
White shorts w/new blue tail shirt. Bl/wh socks,
blue belt and white hat.

SAT. 9TH   3RD ROUND
Blue Tail Shorts w/ yellow new tail shirt. Bl/wh
socks, blue belt and blue hat

Banquet is casual- wear warm-up jacket with uniform.
Bring white and blue sweater and vests.

REMEMBER TO BRING:

PHOTO I.D. TWO HATS (NAVY AND WHITE) SCRUNCHIES, Reebok WIND
SHIRT, UMBRELLA, TURTLENECKS, AND YARDAGE BOOKS.

UCLA WOMEN'S GOLF TEAM

Weekly Schedule

Date	Time	Activity	Location
Mon., Feb. 3,	7 am		
Tu., Feb. 4	1pm		
Wed., Feb. 5	6:45 am		
Th., Feb. 6	1:30 pm		
Fri., Feb. 7	1:30 pm		

Coach Steinmann's thought for the week:
"Pretend (imagine) like a child, and you will find *the magic."*

Something to think about:
"The way a team plays as a whole determines its susccess. You may have the greatest bunch of individual stars in the world, but if they don't play together, the club won't be worth a dime." Babe Ruth

Reminder:
Write in your notebooks.

Palos Verdes Tournament:
Practice round on **Saturday** is at 12:30. Uniform later.
The college-am is on **Sunday**. Breakfast at the PVCC at 9:00 AM. Uniform schedule later.

Teams playing:
SMU, STANFORD, TEXAS, TEXAS A&M, UCLA, USC, WISCONSIN, ARIZONA, ARIZONA ST., IOWA, IOWA ST., MICHIGAN, NEW MEXICO, NEW MEXICO ST., NORTHWESTERN, OHIO, SAN JOSE ST., TULSA.

UCLA WOMEN'S GOLF TEAM

Weekly Schedule

Date	Time	Activity	Location
4/27/98	7:30 am	TEAM MEETING	
4/28/98	1:30 pm	Brentwood, Sand Game practice. Reach green, throw ball in bunker, count strokes from bunker shot . **SAND BOX CHAMPION**	
4/29/98	7:00 am	PRACTICE AT SPAULDING FIELD	
4/30/98	1:30 pm	Hillcrest. In pairs play the par 3's. Use range finder to calculate distances. Play 9 holes from red tees. **CLOSEST TO PIN CONTEST ON EACH HOLE. Mark down the distance on your score card.**	

Coach Steinmann's thought for the week:

The short game is **63** % of your **score.**

Putting is **40%** of your **score.**

Hello Hello Hello! Anybody there?

106

UCLA WOMEN'S GOLF TEAM

Weekly Schedule

Date	Time	Activity	Location
3/3/98	1:30		PRACTICE
WILSHIRE/HILLCREST			
		Short Game	sign up on desk in office who is going where.
3/4/98	7:00	SHORT GAME PRACTICE (BRING OWN BALLS)	WILSHIRE
3/5/98	1:30	PLAY 14 HOLES Qualifier for Betty, Julie and Laura	HILLCREST
3/6/98	6:45	PLAY 9 HOLES Qualifier for Betty, Julie and Laura	BEL AIR
3/9/98	8:00	TEAM MEETING (BRING WEDGES)	RM.116
3/10/98	1:30	PRACTICE ON OWN	
3/11/98	6:00 a.m.	LEAVE FOR L.S.U. /Delta	

Coach Steinmann's thought for the week: "Nobody can intimidate you without your permission."

Something to think about: The only reason to go to the range is to practice targeting. Mechanics are done without a ball in front of a mirror, camera, or teacher to get feedback. As soon as you add a ball and/or target and you are working on mechanics, you have total ambiguity....confusion, confusion, confusion. The brain cannot do both.

KEY ELEMENTS FOR EFFECTIVE LESSONS

1. <u>Attention.</u> Make the environment conducive for learning with no distractions. For example, move to the end of the driving range.

2. <u>Rapport.</u> Develop trust and confidence in your instruction and ability by immediately building rapport. (See chapter on developing rapport.)

3. <u>Keeping it simple</u>. Learning in chunks is critical. Too much and too fast at one time will cause overload and confusion. Motto should be one thing at a time.

4. <u>Attention span</u>. Do not teach through someone's attention span. The brain gets tired.

5. <u>Using words.</u> Be on the same page with the student. The language you use is extremely important. When you say, "down" for example, be sure the students understand the meaning of the word "down". Their perception may be different from yours. Words to be careful of: Through, down, up, aim, around, target, down and through, open, closed, shift, balance, center, hitting area, pull, slice, hook, back swing, wind up, square, *etc*.

6. <u>Feedback.</u> Your advice and comments are important for learning faster, correcting mistakes and motivating. The feedback should be related to learning style. (Auditory, Visual, Kinesthetic).

7. <u>Experiencing.</u> It is the best way to learn. Becoming aware and sensing what they are doing. Does it make sense to the student or non-sense?

8. <u>Modeling</u>. It is necessary. Show them by demonstration, a picture or camera use.

9. <u>**Repetition.**</u> Create ways to allow for repeat performance. Repetitions without interference create habits, good or bad by the way.

10. <u>Imagination.</u> Mental practice doesn't just happen. It is a learned process and develops more with practice. Imagine doing it successfully, vividly, in color, in a suitable environment, *i.e.,* in a crowd using all their senses.

11. <u>**Rehearsal**</u> . Practicing successful outcomes, with eyes open and closed, will build confidence and lessen anxiety.

12. <u>**Presentation.**</u> Instruction must be concise, clear and specific in a positive way.

13. <u>**Teach in the student's dominate sense.**</u> Get out of your dominate sense, (Auditory, Visual, Kinesthetic), and into theirs. They will learn quicker, and instruction will make more sense to them. See chapter on testing.

14. <u>**Remember.**</u> What they do is what they think, or what the brain is processing. Remember also that the worse they think they are at a task, the better they have learned it.

15. <u>Reward.</u> Build self-esteem with sincerity. A pat on the back, a reassuring word, *etc.*

16. **Listen to what they have to say.**

CONFUSION

Overwhelming, overloaded and blow-your-mind are terms one may use to describe confusion. The dictionary describes the word confuse as "a means to make a person so uneasy and bewildered that he cannot think clearly or act sensibly."

When you are confused, you probably have too much unclear information. Most everyone at sometime has experienced confusion from well-meaning teachers, coaches, salesmen, bosses or others. For example, computer experts and golf instructors are famous for this type of behavior. They have their own language and often, without meaning to, overload their students. The result for the inexperienced recipient is overwhelming. Millions of people suffer from this well-meaning activity in everyday life. Most of the time, too much information is confusing. Learning is easier with a one thing at a time approach. "You can't eat an elephant in one bite."[12]

Quicker and easier learning is accomplished in small bits. **Teach in chunks**. Learning one chunk at a time and mastering it before introducing the next chunk can make learning easier, faster, permanent and more fun.

Think back to when you first learned to use a computer. How long did it take you to learn computer language? How about typing on the keyboard, or how to maneuver around the different windows, *etc*? Just to learn how to open and close a document and a file in the beginning was a big step. Imagine someone telling you all of this in one sitting. Or another example would be calling for technical assis-

---

[12] Chuck Hogan

tance with a problem on a computer. You may have found it difficult to follow the technical person's instruction if you are not sure what he/she is even talking about. Your brain goes ballistic, confusion sets in and you either turn off your brain or bite your lip and have them start over slowly.

This happens in teaching any subject, golf or any other sport. It also does not matter if you are young or old. Presenting something in lengthy terms and unfamiliar language will confuse the learner and what the teacher is presenting will be obliterated.

See the cycle of competence in Chapter II.

Here are some tips:
1. Speak clearly.
2. Use words that the learner understands. Remember that the words you use may not mean the same to the student as they mean to you. Explain words that may not be familiar to them.
3. Get feedback. Ask them to repeat the instructions, or ask if they can demonstrate the instructions. What they do is what they got from your instructions.
4. Demonstrate slowly, completely and accurately. You are the model.
5. Use pictures, drawing or charts, *etc.* and relate instruction to other sports or actions that are familiar to the student.
6. Be patient.
7. Show compassion.
8. Use encouragement. Identify what they are doing well.
9. Stay away from words like *don't, wrong, no* and other negative words. The brain does not recognize negatives, so be positive.
10. Control you emotions and they will control theirs.
11. Teach in small increments.
12. Make it fun.

SUGGESTED LESSONS

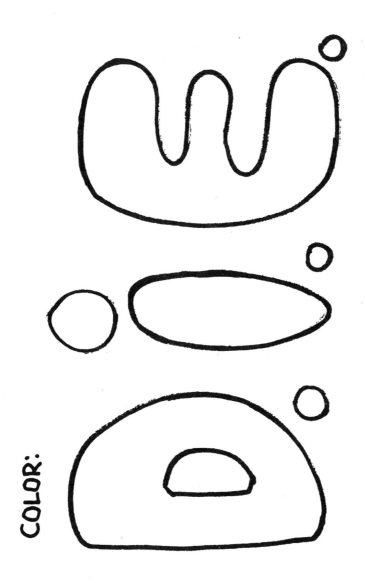

COLOR:

DISTANCE is EVERTHING–

SOMETHING GOOD TO DO WITH PLAYERS

At the top of a piece of paper print this statement:

I am a great person, and I will play well because when I play tournament golf, I am:

Have them list at least 10 things they know about themselves. Then print them up and paste them in their yardage book before a tournament so that they can look at it before every hole.

Here are some examples written by members of the UCLA team:
I am a great person, and I will play well because when I play tournament golf, I am:

Player A
Know how to win.
Dedicated
Don't let anything get in my way of success.
Physically strong
More energy
I know I can be #1
I have a special gift
I have a wonderful family who are 100%
    behind me
Always prepared
I have great mechanical skills
Consistent
I have wonderful teammates and coach
· I believe in myself

Player B
Patient
Focused
Mentally strong
Supportive
Spirited
Thoughtful
Healthy
Stable

Player C

Confident
Mentally tough
Love golf
Have fun on the course
Great swing
Great short game
Awesome putter
Consistent
Know I'll win

Player D

Pay attention to others
Do what I need to do when
   I have to
Have a good attitude on the
   course
Practice efficiently
Don't waste time
Team player
Enjoy playing
Happy
Know that when I get in trouble
   I can get up and down
Focused

SOME IDEAS FOR ACTIVITIES TO DO WITH YOUR TEAM

If you want to teach your team:
- Togetherness
- One person can't do it all,
- We all have to be on the same page,

Here is an idea:

1. Have the whole team stand around a big conference table. Ask if there is anyone in the room who can lift it by themselves. (Of course there is always a dreamer, so let them try with logical safety measure.) When the dreamer is unsuccessful, ask everybody on the count of three to lift the conference table. They will do it easily.

2. Find a rock about three feet in diameter or a raised area of some sort. You could also find a piece of a fence with a ledge and mark off a three-foot section. Ask the team to all stand on the rock together and hold it for one minute. Or, hang onto the fence and each other in the three-foot section for one minute.

How about teaching a team:
- We are only as good as our weakest link.

1. Find a field or open area. Have the entire team hold hands tightly. Have the last person sit on the ground. Have the first person start running with the team following except for the one sitting on the ground. When the team is calmed down, ask for their feelings and interpretations.

Use your imagination and be creative.

With these exercises, you can find the leader, **the one yelling directions**, and accomplish your objectives.

Something to Think About

How precise is Tiger Woods? He said he didn't really hit his seven-iron second shot at No. 17 the way he wanted. "I tried to hit about a one-yard draw there," but it started out about two yards left of where I wanted it."[13]

---

[13] *Los Angeles Times*, Sunday July 23, 2000

CHAPTER IV

Mental Techniques

MOTIVATION

Everybody is motivated all the time, every day, every minute. People do the things they do because they want to, otherwise they would be doing something different. Coaches can guide, direct, encourage, persuade, influence and challenge, but coaches cannot make someone want something. Motivation is a revolving circle. This is the simple version. Find out what they want. What is not working for them and what would the picture look like if everything were working? Have them recognize the choices they have made and what they could do differently to get what they want. Assist them in that direction and praise them for their successes.

The following is an example of what a coach might want to say several weeks before a tournament to direct or influence behavior in "what if" manner.

How could you prepare for the Regional Championships?

What if you prepared for Regionals by thinking about and dreaming every night how you will play, how you will swing, chip, pitch, execute sand shots and putt. Could you dream about how much fun you will have? In your dreams, could you walk through a special pretend door onto the first tee and feel up, ready and confident for competition? Could you see yourself and the team at the end of the tournament standing in front of everybody as the winners? Could you feel what that might be like? Could you picture what you will be wearing and how you will be smiling and what you will be saying to your teammates and your friends? Can you get involved with colors, the feel of the wind, the warmth of the sun? Could you experience the feeling of good shots, the sensation of the ball going into the hole? Maybe you could hear the ball strike the club and listen for the sound of the ball dropping in the cup. What if you hovered over the golf course like a helicopter and pictured each hole, or flew like a bird and inspected each pin placement? Maybe you could be a little puppy in the bottom of the cup that catches the ball going into the hole, or pretend you are an arrow that zings at the bull's-eye, or that you are a camera that sees all or maybe a feather, a cloud or a rainbow, or even a piece of cotton that slowly carries your ball softly onto the green and close to the cup. You could get so involved with how wonderful you will be playing, how happy you will be and how much fun you will be having that automagically, wonderful things happen during the actual event. Wouldn't that be great? Wouldn't that feel absolutely magnificent? Wouldn't you be happy, excited and up? What can you lose? You have time to dream about Regionals and weeks to dream about the Nationals Championships. Dreams do come true to deserving and wonderful people like you. I wonder how many times Tiger dreamed about winning the Masters?

Something to Think About

Something to Think About

The 4 "Ds"

Athletics and life, in fact, are all about the following:

- DISCIPLINE
- DESIRE
- DETERMINATION
- DEDICATION

Doing whatever it takes to get what you want.

The doing and choosing are the important parts.

YOU ARE WHAT YOU THINK YOU ARE.
YOU HAVE WHAT YOU WANT.

You can train your mind to do what ever you want. Your thoughts, your words and what you do express who you really are. If there is something in your life, you want to do or experience, do not just think about it, choose it. Choose it with all your heart. Have a passion for it and take action. For example, it is a false conception when you say, "When I have more money, I will be happy. If I get married then I will be happy. When I get to college, I will be happy. If I get a car, I will be happy. If I play well, then I will be happy." The concept is to be happy first. It is a choice.

When you want to change something, act as if it has already changed. When you put your attention to something, you put energy into it; you act on it, and think about it. What you think about happens. Your life and your actions are a statement of who you are. If what you choose to do is not getting you what you want, then choose to do something else. No one does anything he does not want to do. That is a big statement. Think about it. You can be happy with everything you do if you understand what you do and why you do it.

You can choose to think a certain way. You can train your mind to do whatever you want. The more you train your mind, by choice, the better your chances are of getting what you want. Understand what you do and why you do it. If you don't want it, don't think about it or give it any energy. It is a well-known statement in human potential that "You are 100% responsible for the results in your life on some level." This statement is hard to comprehend for many people and they can find many arguments to prove it false, but if it were not true, your life would be different.

Something to Think About

Use the "**Be, Do, Have** Theory." "**BE** all that you can be," "**DO** whatever it takes," and "You will **HAVE** what you want." There are no limitations, only the ones you put on yourself.

IMAGINATION

Your accomplishments have always been the result of your imagination.

Einstein believed that imagination was more important than knowledge. He was quoted as saying "The brain is like a parachute, it works best when it is open." We would never have had an electric light bulb, the golf club or a spoon, in fact, without someone's imagination. Often necessity is the mother of invention. In order to be creative, you must have an imagination. Creativity and imagination is really how we make golf shots. The more creative we are the more successful we become.

It always seemed to me, that my imagination magnified when I listened to other people talk. Many pictures would dance into my mind. Pictures of other ways to accomplish something or another way to do something or illustrate a point became very clear to me. I often used words blown up like pictures or cartoons to start a lesson or meeting. i.e.–

The lesson today is all about imagination.
Color the word "imagination."

Kids from one to ninety-two like to color with crayons, pencils or pens. Give them permission to do it and they will have fun and learn at the same time. You can make a drawing of a word, a cartoon or let them make their own. Below are a few ideas to get you started.

1. Draw a door to the first tee. Make it as colorful as you like. Pretend that it is a door that you can walk through to the first tee. On the other side is peace, quiet, success and a feeling of being relaxed, in control and at ease. Can you put this in picture form in your mind? Put it on paper. You don't have to be Picasso.

2. Draw a picture of the word "IMAGINATION" or "TRUST" or "PERFORMANCE" or "FOCUS" and it can start a great lesson.

3. Find animals in the clouds on trips.

4. Look at a bunch of flowers in a field or a garden and imagine that they are people. What are they talking about?

5. Watch animals at the zoo and pretend they are people talking about you or your team.

6. Use a cartoon.

7. Look for greeting cards and find appropriate ones you can use.

8. Use magazine illustrations or ones found in a book.

9. Pretend the target is a bank, put a dollar in the bank.

10. Pretend your best friend is standing in the hole ready to catch your ball.

11. Imagine your ball sailing to the target with the wind.

12. Imagine the ball landing in the hole with a puff of smoke.

13. Imagine the flight of the ball like a rainbow with a pot of gold at the end.

14. Imagine your ball a feather floating to the target.

15. Imagine your club a magic wand.

16. Imagine the sound of the ball falling in the hole.

17. Imagine the *ping* when the club strikes the ball.

18. Imagine the sound of a rocket as the ball whistles through the air.

19. Imagine a big black spider on the back of the ball to squash.

20. Imagine the tick tock of your swing.

Use your imagination. Imagine how you can do it. Wonderful pictures will emerge.

Then again, if you want to see **great** imagination, watch a bunch of two-year-olds. Go to a playground or a pre-school and just watch. Children are what they are imagining. They are the nurse, the doctor, the fireman, the pilot and the truck driver. What a great concept when it comes to a sport. You can be Michael Jordan, The Shack, Wayne Gretsky, Jack Nicklaus, Annika Sorenstam, Jackie Joyner Kersee, Michelle Kwan or Tiger Woods. Use your imagination. Pretend.

Pretend that you are confident. Pretend that you are a great putter. Pretend until you become what you pretend. Your imagination will make the difference. You are as good as you make up your mind to be. You are as good as what you imagine. The sooner you come to believe in the power of your imagination, the easier golf and coaching will become.

The whole crux of human intelligence rests on imagination.

SO DO ALL GOLF SHOTS.

THE COPYCAT BRAIN

Watch children play and imitate the actions of others. Do you know a child who is the spitting image of a parent in they way they talk or walk? If you have observed this, then you may have wondered why this is so. The fact is that children and all of us, in fact, learn by imitating or modeling. Research reveals that imitation is a natural tool for developing and learning. So often when we find ourselves on unfamiliar ground trying to master a part of the golf swing or a new activity, we learn by watching someone else and then following his or her lead, good or bad. Learning this way, we rely on a powerful instinctive talent for imitation. This happens starting at birth and continues our whole life. This built-in mechanism allows us to imitate movement and expressions we see in other people. As an experiment, stick your tongue out close to the face of a three-month-old and watch him/her imitate you.

The same parts of the brain that send commands to our muscles when we act also are able to recognize the same actions when performed by others. Once you understand how the brain is set up to learn, you can understand better ways to coach and teach. As a basic neural process, imitation itself may be as old as monkey-see and monkey-do. We have special mirror neurons in our brain that act when we imitate.

So taking into consideration the above information, which is adapted from the research of UCLA neuroscientist Marco Iacobone and his colleagues in Italy and Germany, it is important to realize that what you do is what your students and athletes will do. That goes for parents as well, because in the scheme of things, parents are our first role models before teachers and coaches appear. If coaches want to know how athletes are likely to behave, or what athletes are going to be like, they need to take a good look at the parents. Understanding this information about how people learn and using it in the developing process of your students, will make you a better coach and teacher.

Let me tell you a little story which relates to this concept. One day last summer, I was playing golf with three gentlemen. One of them, Richard, was a good friend of mine, who was a student of the golf swing and very knowledgeable. He is forever teaching his friends and whoever will listen to him. His swing is not the picture perfect swing, but it works for him. He does not give information accurately or most efficiently, but his heart is in the right place. As the golf game came around to the 18th hole, one of the other gentlemen playing in our group, who was new to the sport and who had almost the **identical** swing as Richard and the same flaws, asked me a question about his golf swing. I asked him who his teacher was. He said Richard. What I thought at the moment was "How amazing, monkey-see and monkey-do."

Antidote: be careful who you watch.

Note: Fact – The Copy Cat Brain and being in the zone are directly related. There is a biological function chemically happening in the brain.

MUSIC TO MY EARS

Since all performance is analog, that means that any kind of athletic endeavor is accomplished with a continuous motion. This continuous motion in athletics is aided by music, which in itself is a continuous motion. In golf, it is important to have a good rhythm. It is especially true for auditory learners. Research has found that you remember the last songs you hear on the way to the golf course. Haven't you at some time had a tune stuck in your head and it just wouldn't leave? It is important that you also hear music that complements your swing. It is a good idea to record music that fits your swing. Find five songs that put you in your rhythm or flow. When you hear a song or tune that you think goes with your swing, stop wherever you are and swing a pretend club to feel if it is the right song for your swing. Record all five songs on one tape. Play these songs through your headset or on your car stereo on the way to the golf course. Do not let someone else's rhythm spoil your day.

I guarantee this will help your athletes. Getting people to do this is the problem, but **you can insist**.

Note: I also guarantee it will be much quieter in the van on the way to the course and the coaches can concentrate better on their driving skills.

WHAT IS CONFIDENCE?

- It's an image or thought.
- It's a feeling.
- It's knowing that you have prepared yourself to the best of your ability.
- Your swing will hold up no matter what.
- Your hold has just the right feel.
- You are feeling relaxed, calm and aggressive.
- You played the course. You have a game plan.
- It's a positive thought.
- It's believing.
- It's a feeling of comfort, ease and rightness.
- It's focused.
- It's feeling physically flexible and in good shape.

Add your own thoughts. Ask your students to make their own list.

FOCUS AND CONCENTRATION

Concentration is what you're a focusing on. It is what you are thinking. It is difficult to focus over long periods of time. The brain needs a rest. You can focus long enough, however, to go through your routine and hit the ball at a target. It is easy to focus on something that is fun or something you like. At other times, you will need willpower. You must be more diligent and make a conscious effort to focus. During your focus period, you must stay in control of your concentration. Your emotions have to step aside and anything else that gets in the way of your attention and intention. Practicing will enable you to get better.

POTENTIAL - INTERFERENCE= EQUALS PERFORMANCE

LIST YOUR INTERFERENCES

PRACTICING FOCUS OR CONCENTRATION

Pick an object. Focus on the object and stare at it looking at it's shape, color, size, texture and shape. Imagine what it would look like from the other side. Stare at it until you are mesmerized, which, by the way is a form of hypnosis. Then pick another object and do the same thing. Get so involved with the object that you can't see or hear anything else. You can also do this with sounds. You could concentrate so much that it even goes in and out of focus. What do you think would happen if you did this with the target? What if the target was so clear to you and you were so completely involved and connected to it that the ball could not go anywhere else but right to it. Is that possible? Maybe! Give it a go. What can you lose?

Something to Think About

If you are trying to learn to do something new, focus on the behavior, *i.e.* the position of the hands, the wind up, the athletic stance, *etc.*

If you are working on distance, trajectory, accuracy or direction, *etc.*, focus on the outcomes or results.

There is a difference, and it is not possible to do both at the same time. Trying to do both creates confusion and learning is difficult.

STRESS AND ANXIETY

Stress is defined as a person's response to their environment, a threat, a feeling of helplessness, fear, distrust or anger. Stress and anxiety are both states of mind just like fear, confidence, happy, hypochondriac, depression, *etc.* States of mind define how we relate to golf, life, teaching or coaching. They define your personality. Pressure comes from wondering what will people think of me. "If I miss this shot, what will my coach think?" "If I have a poor score, what will my parents think?" "If I don't make this putt, what will my team think of me?" "If the team doesn't do well what will the teams think?" You get the picture. You put pressure on yourself by what you are thinking. It is a choice you are making. Nobody has control of your mind other than you. Choose to think in a way that assist you instead of making a choice that gets in your way. We always move toward pleasure and away from pain. When we move toward and away at the same time, we create pressure, frustration and anxiety. When fears interfere with our performance, and it happens to all of us, make it you friend. Learn to relax and stay focused. Think about how you got there, how well you prepared and that you deserve to be successful. It takes practice and willpower. Great amounts of pressure eventually lead to disillusionment and burnout.

Something to Think About

"We make real that to which we pay attention."

Conversations with God

CHAPTER V

Practice Preparation and Playing the Game

PRACTICE

I wonder sometimes why people go to the driving range, the field or the court to practice. I believe their intentions are good, but many times they are non-productive. Let us take a closer look at why, what and how to practice.

Why?

Because of the old saying, practice makes perfect or
    perfect practice makes perfect.
You get better at what you want to do if you practice.
Practice is a repetition process that assists in forming habits.

What?

It seems everybody knows what to practice.
You recognize faults from statistics, from mistakes, from lack of
    execution and poor results.

How?

How to practice is the big factor.

ALL ABOUT PRACTICE

Most of us believe that if we want to be good at anything, we have to practice. And it is true. Why? Because practice makes perfect or perfect practice makes perfect, so the saying goes. You get better at what you do if you practice. Practice is a process that assists in forming habits. Most of us know what to practice. We can discover this from our statistics or from our experiences. However, how to practice is a different story. Let's take a good look at how to practice.

1. Efficient practice takes discipline. In fact, golf or any sport is all about discipline. It takes discipline to do whatever it takes to be successful. It takes discipline to practice efficiently. So, what are the steps in practicing with discipline?

2. This daily procedure is how you do it:
   • Warm up your body
   • Warm up your mind
   • Decide what to practice
   • Maintain your intention (your goals set for that day)
   • Maintain your attention (keep your focus)
   • Don't try. Experience, adjust, experience
   • Isolate desired outcome
   • Evaluate only your desired outcome (one at a time)
   • Practice, Rest, Practice (don't practice through your attention span)
   • Practice success (Don't keep doing the same thing over and over if it is not working)
   • Anchor success with an emotional response (pump your fist, smile or just say "yes," *etc.*)

- Practice mechanics or practice golf. (You can't do both at the same time.)
- List successes.

Something to Think About

As a coach, teacher or parent, adaptability, imagination and your ability to make wise choices are your most valuable assets.

Something to Think About

With enough practice on the short game a golfer can be turned into a scoring machine.

An example of a typical week of practice on the golf team:

The following is what the team would do if they were not going to a tournament. NCAA rules state that practice with the coach present is limited to 20 hours per week which includes meetings and workouts. Coach is present at 95% of the practices.

Of course the evenings are free to study and relax.

The Mountain Gate Country Club is open to practice on the range at any time.

Physical training is two to three hours a week.

Monday:
Team meeting at 7:00 AM – "Mental Training," discussions and announcements including schedule for the week or short game practice with coach, or Practice at 6:30 AM at Bel Air Country Club

Classes in the late morning and early afternoon

45 minutes to an hour in the training room – exercise.

Tuesday:
Classes in the morning

Golf practice in the afternoon at 1:30 PM at Brentwood Country Club or Riviera Country Club.

Wednesday:
Practice at Wilshire Country Club. Classes in the afternoon.

45 minutes to an hour in the training room – exercise.

Thursday:
Classes in the morning.

Practice at 1:30 PM at Hillcrest Country Club

Friday:
Practice at 6:30 AM at Bel Air Country Club or short game practice at Mountain Gate Country Club or Vista Valencia or free time to do whatever.

Physical training again in the training room.

Weekend:
Free to practice or do whatever.

Other practice areas: Palos Verdes CC, weekends and weekdays, call club

Riviera CC range practice weekdays, call club

Wilshire CC range practice Wednesdays

Mountain Gate CC any day

Hillcrest CC, call club

GAMES AND DRILLS

**The following are a few games and drills to get you started.
Build your own library.**

PUTTING IS 43% OF YOUR SCORE

Putting exercises:

1. Right hand
2. Left hand
3. Eyes closed
4. No take away-push the ball
5. Look at the hole
6. Between shafts
7. Listen for the sound
8. Putt to smaller objects
9. Ladder Drill with 5 tees at different lengths
10. Fringe putting-putt to different parts of the fringe for distance
11. Games
12. Putt in the dark to a light source
13. Putt on carpet, linoleum, sidewalk, etc.
14. One ball, different holes just like real golf
15. Putt, anchor the good.
16. Practice making putts not missing putts.
17. Isolate your goals.

This mini-course was designed to test your chipping and putting skills.

Hole	Activity	Balls	Par	Player
1	25 ft Putt	2	4	
2	45 ft Putt	2	4	
3	Lob Pitch	2	5	
4	Long Breaking Putt	2	4	
5	10-12 ft Putt	2	3	
6	Chip from Rough	2	5	
7	Long Putt	2	4	
8	Long Chip & Run	2	4	
9	5 ft & 8 ft Putts	2	3	
	TOTAL		36	

To attempt par, play two balls per hole, as indicated on your score sheet, until both are holed out. Count total number of strokes.

Place all balls, except on hole #6, where the ball must be dropped.

This mini-course was designed to test your skill in short approach shots.

Hole	Activity	Balls	Par	Player
1	Med Range Pitch	3	6	
2	Pitch from Bunker	3	6	
3	Pitch over Bunker	3	7	
4	Short Bunker Shot	3	6	
5	Long Bunker Shot	3	6	
6	Long Approach	3	5	
	TOTAL		36	

To attempt par, hit the number of balls indicated. Do not putt out. Use the scoring system below.

SCORING

0 = Ball in hole
1 = Ball in small circle(2 putter lengths)
2 = Ball in large circle(flagstick & 1/2)
3 = Ball on green
4 = Ball on fringe
5 = Ball in rough
6 = Ball in bunker

This mini-course was designed to test your chipping and putting skills.

Hole	Activity	Balls	Par	Player
1	25 ft Putt	2	4	
2	45 ft Putt	2	4	
3	Lob Pitch	2	5	
4	Long Breaking Putt	2	4	
5	10-12 ft Putt	2	3	
6	Chip from Rough	2	5	
7	Long Putt	2	4	
8	Long Chip & Run	2	4	
9	5 ft & 8 ft Putts	2	3	
	TOTAL		36	

To attempt par, play two balls per hole, as indicated on your score sheet, until both are holed out. Count total number of strokes.

Place all balls, except on hole #6, where the ball must be dropped.

This mini-course was designed to test your skill in short approach shots.

Hole	Activity	Balls	Par	Player
1	Med Range Pitch	3	6	
2	Pitch from Bunker	3	6	
3	Pitch over Bunker	3	7	
4	Short Bunker Shot	3	6	
5	Long Bunker Shot	3	6	
6	Long Approach	3	5	
	TOTAL		36	

To attempt par, hit the number of balls indicated. Do not putt out. Use the scoring system below.

SCORING

0 = Ball in hole
1 = Ball in small circle(2 putter lengths)
2 = Ball in large circle(flagstick & 1/2)
3 = Ball on green
4 = Ball on fringe
5 = Ball in rough
6 = Ball in bunker

<u>SHORT GAME TEAM CONTEST</u>.....Name:_____

Ladder Drill: Contestant must putt from the tee, (both from the uphill tee as well as downhill), the goal is to get a ball to stop in each of the four ladder steps. The perfect score is eight, but the contestant can take as many putts as needed to complete the goal of one ball in each of the ladder steps.

SCORE:

_____

_____	_____	_____	_____
1ST Step	2nd Step	3rd Step	4th Step

Total Score

_____	_____	_____	_____
57th Step	8th Step	7th Step	8th Stpe

Around the World: The goal of this drill is for the contestant to hole a putt from each of the eight tees positioned around the cup. The contestant gets two chances from each tee to hole a putt. If the contestant fails to hole the putt after two attempts, he must start over from the original starting point. The total putts it takes the contestant to complete the cycle is the contestants score for this drill.

_____

Total Score

PuttingLine Drill: The goal of this drill is to putt a ball into each of the three designated areas. The perfect score is three, but the player must count all putts until he gets a ball to come to rest in each of the three areas.

_____

Total Score

_____	_____	_____
30'	40'	50'

Chipping Line Drill: This is the same as above, except with chipping.

_____

Total Score

_____	_____	_____
20'	30'	40'

Sand Line Drill: This is the same as above, except with sand shots.

_____

Total Score

_____	_____	_____
20'	30'	40'

_____ **Total Score, (Add all five drills).**

148

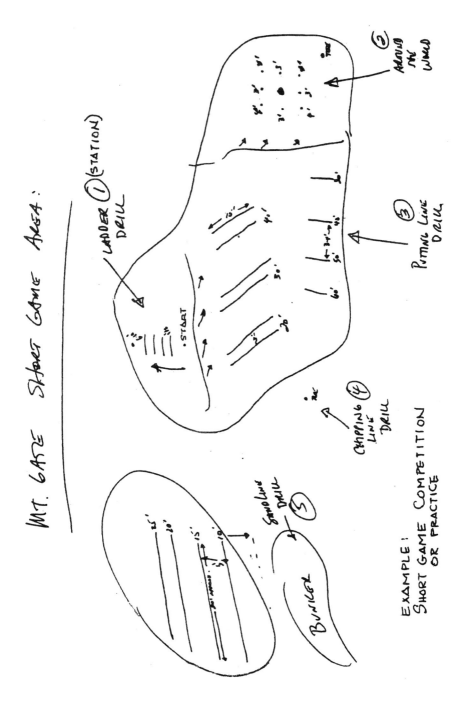

MT. GATE SHORT GAME AREA :

LADDER ① (STATION) DRILL

START

② MOVING THE WORLD

③ PUTTING LINE DRILL

④ CHIPPING LINE DRILL

⑤ SAND LINE DRILL

BUNKER

EXAMPLE :
SHORT GAME COMPETITION
OR PRACTICE

149

Exercise: Three clubs ... 3W, 7 Iron, Putter. Play 18 holes.

1.   What was your experience during this exercise?

2.   Was it fun?

3.   What did you learn? ("Every limitation is a unique piece of learning.")

4.   Did your experience change at all during the 18 holes? If so, how?

5.   Did you become aware of anything different?

6.   How was your attitude? To what degree did you participate in the exercise?

7.   How did you play considering the limitations?

Target drill

Set targets out 25, 40 and 55 yards and alternately hit one shot at a time to each. This will help you relate distance to arm motion, rather than tension and effort. It will let you develop judgment, not just technique.

Hit balls with eyes closed

This drill is designed to show that you don't have to watch the ball fixedly and become ball-bound. It also helps you develop good pace in your arm swing. Just try to make a smooth motion back and forth to the target, and you'll strike a pretty good shot. If, with your eyes closed, you consciously try to hit the ball, you'll miss it.

Strike short shots at pie plates

Staple or tape paper pie plates onto dowels at varying heights and practice chipping and pitching to these targets. This helps you relate arm swing on the short shots to both trajectory and distance.

Chip with an extra-long club

To keep your left hand and wrist firm on the short shots around the green, practice with a special club. Cut the grip cap off an old chipping or pitching club, find an old golf shaft and stick it in the shaft of the club. Now grip the club normally and practice your short shots. The extension of the shaft will force you to keep your left wrist firm and your hands ahead of the ball going through the shot. Your ribs will tell you if you don't.

Anti-shank board drill

This is a by-product of the board drill for the full swing. Place your two-by-four parallel to the target line and set the ball so there is no more than half an inch from the toe of the club to the board. Start hitting little chip shots, then gradually longer pitches. The board prevents the club from going outside the line and thus keeps you from shanking or hitting the ball with the hosel.

Chip over bag

Put your golf bag 18 inches in front of a ball. Tap down on the ball with no follow-through and pop the ball over the bag. This creates a descending blow. If you try to scoop the ball, either your clubhead or the ball or both will hit the bag. The pitfall is that you may tend to throw the club with the right hand and jam it into the ground.

Slap drill

Open the face of your sand wedge 90 degrees so the leading edge is parallel to your target line. Then make a few swings with a very steep, descending blow. Feel the club slap the sand and bounce out. This develops the sensation of the flange or bottom hitting first, instead of the leading edge. Then gradually close the clubface with each succeeding swing until you no longer feel the bounce and are getting drag from the leading edge. This further develops the different sensations you'll get from the different shots you must play in the sand.

STATISTICS

Let's talk about statistics for a moment. Statistical programs are especially helpful because of the feedback they produce. Some people, especially left brained people, can be a slave to statistics. Putting too much emphasis on statistics may not produce positive results. However, in order to point you in a direction, make different choices, and set different goals, each person should keep statistics. What direction your practice sessions need to take is an example. If your putting statistics are high, then you will want to practice your putting and so on. Statistics over a length of time let you know where you are weak and where your strengths lie.

Most college programs use the statistical program that Golf Stat has designed. It is a very good system and gives excellent feedback. Mark Lasch has many years of experience is designing statistical programs for amateur golfers. It can be especially helpful for college golf teams. Mark has varying levels of involvement in his program. He can be reached by calling Golf Stat at 309-828-6430.

Following these paragraphs are examples of the program. As you will see, it can give you statistics about putting, fairways hit, greens hit, sand save percentage, up and down percentages etc. It can even tell you how you do in three-hole increments in the 18 holes for three days. This statistic for example can give you feedback as to how you start, how you finish and all in-between. The awareness you gain from this particular statistic may lead you to solving a problem. For example, if your scores are high on an average for the first three holes, maybe you aren't ready to play. Maybe you were in too much of hurry, or maybe you didn't have enough time to warm up, *etc*. On the other hand, if your scores on an average are high in the middle of the round, maybe you are hungry, tired or have lost concentration. Becoming aware is the key.

Once you have enough statistics, you can compare yourself to the better teams or individuals or even to the professional players. Stats of college players can be obtained through Golf Stat, and statistics for professional players can be found in golf magazines or on the Internet. See the average statistics following for the LPGA as of the writing of this book. However, I do not believe it changes much over time; only individuals change positions according to what they want.

Statistics and their comparisons can be a motivating tool.

THE IMPORTANCE OF STATISTICS

Coach Steinmann has asked me to write my opinion of the importance of statistics for coaching college golf. Statistics can be a valuable tool in analyzing a person's game. I personally enjoy talking to coaches about players who I have never seen play and see if I can accurately define the type of player they are by looking at their numbers. It is amazing how much you can define about a player by their statistics.

The number one comment we get from college coaches is that their players can look at their statistics and often start practicing their weaknesses without being told. As coaches tell me, "When it's in black and white, they (players) don't need to be told what to work on." This makes practice time more efficient and more importantly coaches don't have to waste time convincing players of their deficiencies.

During a college golf tournament, a coach can only witness a certain percentage of shots taken by their players. Statistics can give the coach a chance to go over each players round and analyze their tournament without having seen much of their play. One thing we do is monitor many negative statistics. Where is the player missing the fairway? Where are they missing the greens? The answer to these questions can often lead the player or coach to a determination of either a swing problem or a course management problem. Defining the problem is the first step to fixing it.

Statistics allow coaches and players to set goals. Golf is a game broken down into certain component parts. Tee shots, fairway shots, short game shots, and putting are the component parts of the game. Statistics give players feedback to compare them against players on their own team and players on other teams.

Some schools use statistics simply to allow their Sports Information Department to have more information on their team. They like to use it to promote their golf programs. Different coaches use statistics for different reasons. That is one of the reasons that Golfstat has always offered different levels of service on our statistical services.

There are some cautions that I always mention about statistics. Numbers need to be presented in an understandable format. I have been a vocal critic of professional statistics because they are presented without much thought. As an example, greens hit is regulation are presented as a percentage. Now let me ask you, have you ever known anyone who ever walked off the course and said, "I hit 67% of the greens". Of course, not, instead they would say they hit 12 greens (67% of 18). Greens in regulation should be presented as a number. We know there are 18 holes on a golf course. This number is fixed. Therefore, greens in regulation should be presented as a number not a percentage. In our college statistics we present them both ways simply because the players also want to compare themselves to the professional players. I don't have as much of a problem with fairways hit being a percentage because you have a varying number of fairways (depending upon the number of Par 3's), but since the majority of golf courses have 14 fairways we also show how many fairways a player hits out of every 14 non-Par 3 tee shots. When you look at the professional statistics take them for what they are: media driven information that is worthless from an analytical point of view.

So, what statistics are important?

On short game statistics, the majority of short game save opportunities are not from the sand so it only makes sense to monitor both sand saves and non-sand saves then analyzing a players game. Putting statistics are also an important element to the overall effectiveness of the player's short game. We show a number of different putting statistics, but the two most informational are average number of 4-putt greens and putting par. Putting par is a great statistic that determines the difference between how many putts a player did have versus how many they should have. How many they should have is based upon how many greens they hit. The formula is 2 putts on every green they hit plus 1 putt on every green that they miss. As an example: If a player hits 10 greens they should have

10 x 2 plus 8 x 1 or 28 putts. If they actually had 30 putts their putting par would be +2.

One reason I like putting par is that it can also be used to analyze where a player is losing their shots. If a player is averaging 6 over par and their putting par is +2, they are losing their other 4 shots from tee to green in some way.

We have also created some pre-determined analysis statistics. These statistics take the numbers and manipulate them to tell the story. One such statistic is the Ham and Egg statistic. This statistic shows how a player is making their pars and birdies. Are they making them in regulation (hitting a lot of greens)?

I also like to look at a players scoring average on Par 3, Par 4, and Par 5 holes. Those relationships can define a player's style of play and help a coach approach how each of his players should approach each golf course they play.

One final caution on statistics. Statistics need to be a post round exercise. I have had many coaches tell me that one of the most important times of the statistical process is when the players fill out their statistical sheets after the round. It acts as a good exercise in going over the round. However, a player should never concentrate on statistics during a round. Make your score and then use statistics to analyze the how and why after you have walked off the 18th hole.

Written by Mark Lasch
Golfstat
PO Box 399
Bloomington, IL 61702-0399

Tour Stats - Women

Scoring	**70.01**
Putting	**29.19**
GIR	**78.4**
Sand Saves	**56.7**
Distance	**263**

Example of two different college teams:

	National Ranking 4th	National Ranking 15th
Scoring average	75.71	78.62
Number pars per round	11.07	9.30
Bogies per round	4.19	6.05
Double Bogies per round	.60	.73
Putts on Greens in regulation	1.899	2.013
3 putt greens %	.97	2.16
Average putts	30.53	33.85
Putts/pars	2.30	5.11
Non sand saves %	.565	.347
Sand saves %	.363	.198
Fairways %	.722	.778
Greens hit %	.57	.598
Green hit within 15' %	.181	.231
Par 3 in regulation %	.55	.622

1996 STATISTICAL COMPARISON [College, Futures Tour,LPGA]

Scoring Average Comparison

	COLLEGE	FUTURES	LPGA
1	71.50	72.12	70.32
2	71.83	72.14	70.47
3	72.44	72.50	70.87
4	72.56	72.62	70.94
5	74.22	73.06	71.35
6	74.35	73.15	71.37
7	74.58	73.24	71.41
8	74.71	73.44	71.43
9	74.79	73.50	71.49
10	74.92	73.50	71.57

Greens Hit in Regulation

	COLLEGE	FUTURES	LPGA
1	0.718	0.778	0.738
2	0.718	0.722	0.727
3	0.716	0.750	0.720
4	0.694	0.710	0.711
5	0.694	0.699	0.709
6	0.671	0.683	0.709
7	0.667		0.708
8	0.654		0.708
9	0.646		0.705
10	0.642		0.702

Putts per Round

	COLLEGE	FUTURES	LPGA
1	30.11	27.70	29.27
2	30.13	28.33	29.38
3	30.33	28.93	29.45
4	30.33	29.10	29.49
5	30.36	29.13	29.49
6	30.43	29.67	29.68
7	30.44		29.70
8	30.50		29.71
9	30.58		29.72
10	30.64		29.74

Driving Accuracy

	COLLEGE	FUTURES	LPGA
1	0.937	0.833	0.820
2	0.905	0.821	0.816
3	0.903	0.821	0.807
4	0.902	0.820	0.806
5	0.899	0.819	0.803
6	0.891	0.819	0.797
7	0.887	0.801	0.786
8	0.884	0.791	0.786
9	0.881	0.789	0.783
10	0.881	0.789	0.781

Sand Saves

	COLLEGE	FUTURES	LPGA
1	0.675		0.577
2	0.667		0.561
3	0.625		0.534
4	0.615		0.531
5	0.571		0.527
6	0.571		0.520
7	0.571		0.519
8	0.571		0.517
9	0.571		0.515
10	0.570		0.507

Driving Distance

	LPGA
1	262.3
2	255.6
3	255.5
4	254.1
5	252.7

****

		LPGA
		218.1
Worst 5 (shortest 5)		217.4
on LPGA Tour 176-180		216.1
		214.4
		210.1

UP & DOWN PERCENTAGE (BY HANDICAP)

HDCP.	# OF ATTEMPTS	SAND	PITCHING	CHIPPING	PUTTER	TOTAL
PGA TOUR	680	51%	53%	79%	93%	67%
PLUS/ZERO	205	38%	48%	72%	84%	60%
1-10	639	16%	33%	35%	78%	35%
11-20	284	8%	20%	23%	47%	23%
21-30	698	8%	17%	26%	45%	22%
31 & OVER	164	1%	3%	25%	40%	14%

3-TOUR COMPARISON (AVE. PLAYER – 1993)

	PGA	SENIOR	LPGA
FAIRWAYS	68%	68%	68%
GREENS	66%	66%	62%
DISTANCE	260	254	224
PUTTS	29.6	29.9	30.5
SAND SAVES	52%	46%	39%
BIRDIES	18%	17%	—
SCORING	71.6	72.1	73.1

A research of 9000 rounds of college play
resulted in the following conclusion:

**Greens in regulation
and putts per round
are the two main
factors that influence
a player's scoring
average, accounting
for 93% of overall
score.**

Short-game instruction

The short game includes shots made with a swing that is less than full.

Since most golfers take more short-game strokes than full-swing strokes during an average round, improving your short game is the best way to lower your scores.

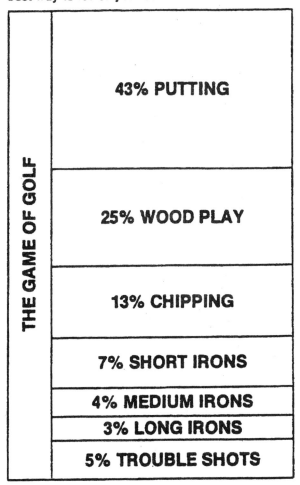

THE GAME OF GOLF

43% PUTTING

25% WOOD PLAY

13% CHIPPING

7% SHORT IRONS

4% MEDIUM IRONS

3% LONG IRONS

5% TROUBLE SHOTS

A Statistical Look at the Game (from a study of 1,000 players ranging from beginners to touring pros).

BETTER APPROACHES TO LOWER SCORING

By - Therese Hession

Most average to above average golfers tend to rely on the perfect shot approaching greens rather than the reality of their average shot! This can make a tremendous difference in scoring over a 3 or 4 day competition. For example, if the average player hits a 6 iron 150 yards on 'good' shot with a little release and roll, it is imperative they are honest with themselves on how often do they really hit it 'good'! Honestly one out of 10 is probably pretty close to reality. A more truthful percentage for what a very 'acceptable' shot hit with that 6 iron would probably go 142-147 yards. If you hit this 'acceptable' 6 iron 75% of the time why not club up a half club so the majority of these shots will be between 147 and 152 yards?

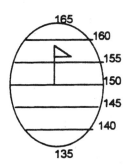

This cuts the average distance for first putts some 15 feet! Our 'best hits' which may travel 152 to 157 yards probably occur only 1 of 10 times will go no further than 21 feet past the hole. Our 'missed shots' which will probably occur the remaining 15% of the time will

162

now find the front of the green instead of relying on a chip shot. It is critical to know carry yardage as well as total yardage so that you can be as accurate as possible with your distances. Weather conditions may also effect these averages on a daily basis as well as the severity of the green.

Along the lines of being truthful with yourself; how about considering the day you have going? For the sake of this presentation, I will describe 3 types of days - an 'A' day, a 'B' day, and a 'C' day. This is by no means forcing one into a limiting mold, but just a truthful analogy of where a player should play to maximize their individual potential. An 'A' day is one where you can't do anything wrong—you are getting every break and feel good over all shots. A 'B' day is your average day where you are doing fairly well, but still not hitting it perfect. A 'C' day is one where you are really struggling and you just can't control much of anything. These days you need to allow as much room as possible for error. Before teeing off it is critical to decide your strategy to approach each green and to adjust your thinking accordingly.

The average green can generally be broken down into 3 areas: red light, yellow light and green light areas. A red light area must be approached very cautiously and only when you're in full control of our game on an 'A' day.

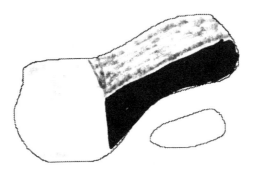

This red light hole location has not much room for error and the penalty for missing the shot is greater than the reward for hitting it perfectly. A hole location in a yellow light area must be approached cautiously as it has a limited amount of room for error. There still may be a difficult putt or chip/bunker shot if not performed at least above average. Hole locations in a yellow light area should only be approached directly on an A or B day. The remainder of the green is a green light area. Hole locations in these areas are readily accessible on nearly every day we play. Green light areas give us the most room for error and generally no penalty for most any shot we will hit. These are the only areas of the green we should aim for on a 'C' day whether the pin is there or not! The average player will save several shots per nine if they are honest with themselves and play within their abilities. On a day when a player's rhythm and timing are not quite there, a player can get back in their rhythm quicker by hitting to green light areas and hitting several greens in a row. This gives you more room for error and takes the pressure off hitting approach shots perfectly. As the confidence resurfaces you may soon move into more familiar rhythm for the remainder of the round rather than having your day be a lost cause!

A player may also break the red, yellow and green areas of approaches down by the club they are approaching the green. Fairway woods and long irons should be hit to green light areas regardless of the hole location. Mid irons can be aimed at yellow light areas if you are having a 'A' or 'B' day, and short irons may be aimed to red light locations only if the player is having an 'A' day.

With a little extra thinking execution can be made a bit easier and the results will surely follow.

THE AIMING PROCESS

AIM WITH YOUR BRAIN

Aiming at a target is intrinsic in every sport. The basketball player aims at the basket, the quarterback aims at his receiver and the archer aims at the bullseye. It is no different in golf. Learning how to aim is a basic step in any sport. Great athletes do it instinctively, but when it comes to golf 90% of golfers do not know how to aim.

The target is a very specific place and more so when it comes to putting. So let's explore how to **AIM WITH YOUR BRAIN**, and incorporate it in a pre shot routine that, by the way, is good for every club in your bag. You should also remember that there could be some slight deviations in this routine to suit your personal preference

AIM THEN ALIGN
That's the first rule. So many people do it backwards. They align first then aim. To consistently be successful at reaching your target, you must aim first.

The second rule. You must aim before every shot in golf even on the practice range as long as you have a target. It takes discipline to do it every time. Golf is all about discipline. You must practice aiming over and over until it becomes a habit, and you automatically do it without thinking.

The following is the pre-shot routine.
1. Stand behind the ball balanced on both feet. Look at the target with both eyes level as you do in every other aspect of your life. Note: The target may not be the hole. Depending on the break (the slope of the green) the target may be inches or feet to the right or left of the hole.

2. You may take practice swings, if you choose, standing behind your ball, and <u>looking at your target</u> in order to get a feel of what you see. Or, you may take practice swings beside the ball and then go back behind the ball in order to aim.

3. When the target is crystal clear in your mind, walk up to the ball **looking at the ball.** No peeking at the target.

4. Place the putter behind the ball and let the putter aim. **Trust that this will happen.** Your brain is amazing. It will assist you perfecting your aim.

5. Now and only now do you take your **stance according to your putter.** In other words, **align** your feet, hips and shoulders perpendicular to the leading edge of the putter. You should feel comfortable.

6. At this point you can take another look at your target, but **for distance only.** Do not change the aim. **Trust.** If you are uncomfortable, start over.

7. Now putt with a pendulum motion, and go get the ball out of the hole.

8. **This advice will assist 90% of golfers, however, with some golfers, there may be extenuating circumstances that prevent accuracy of this aiming process.**

Get target-oriented when you play golf. Fall in love with the target. Get so involved with the target that the ball has little chance of going anywhere else. Always find the smallest target you can see. For example a piece of grass on the cup, the right side of a tree in the distance or the left edge of a chimney on a house, *etc.* Narrow your target to the smallest point. Remember it is not just out there somewhere. Think about someone shooting an arrow. Does he/she go for the bull's eye or the barrel of hay? Your chances are much better when you focus on something small and specific. Learn how to aim. It is crucial in hitting a golf ball to a target. I have noticed that with many golfers the perception of the hole or target is right or left, sometimes as much as a foot especially in putting and yards in longer shots. What happens when you misaim is significant. You compensate in your swing or stroke to get the ball to go where you want it to go. Your brain recognizes the misaiming and directs you to compensate. The majority of mistakes come from misaiming. Learn how to aim. Do what good putters do.

The following will assist you and your student athletes in the aiming process. You must remember that aiming at a target has to do with perception. The hole in their head and the hole in the ground may not be the same thing. Once they know how to aim, all there is ... is distance.

First:

1. Know their learning dominance so that you can talk to them in terms that they will understand easily. (See Sensory Dominance worksheet in chapter II.)

2. Know which eye is dominant. There are several methods to detect the dominant eye. A simple way, but not completely accurate, is to ask them to wink. The dominant eye is usually the opposite eye. They need to use their dominant eye to place the putter or club behind the ball in the aiming process described in the previous paragraphs. Turning the head slightly toward the target with the eyes on the target line for right eye dominate people or turning the head slightly away from the target for left eyed people will assist in aiming.

3. Knowing if they are right- or left-footed (which foot do they usually use to start up steps), and right- or left-eared (where do they usually put the telephone) helps in understanding their preferences. It is the right eared, right footed and left eyed person that has the ideal situation for aiming.

Second:

After watching students putt several times; you can give them feedback with the following information and/or use the "in-sighter" which can be purchased by calling 1-800-345-4245.

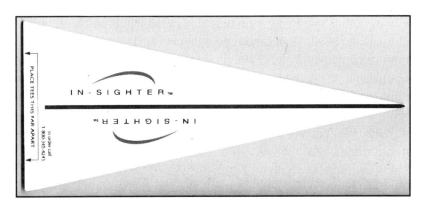

The in-sighter's base is placed along the putter's leading edge, after the student aims and sets the putter. The in-sighter points to where the putter is aimed and any discrepancies can easily be pointed out to the student by leaving the in-sighter in place and taking the putter away.

To correct misaiming:

If you find, that they consistently place the club or putter facing to the right of the target, you can do several things.

- Tell them that they are aiming right. This may correct the process on the next attempt. If this doesn't help, have them look at the target (aim), walk up to the ball looking at the ball and stand facing the ball with their body open to the target as they place their putter or club behind the ball. Then they can take their stance according to the leading edge of the club or putter.
- Or, experiment with the student holding the putter or club in the right hand as they approach the ball.
- One of these should correct aiming to the right of the target.

If you find that the student is consistently aiming to the left of the target, try the following.

- Tell them that they are aiming left. This may correct aiming on the next attempt.
- Or, have them stand square or closed to the target when they place the club behind the ball in the aiming process.
- Or, experiment with the student holding the club in the left hand as they approach the ball or have them hold it with both hands.

If your student or athlete randomly and consistently aims right and left, it is extremely difficult to assist them.

Correct aiming is part of the pre shot routine. It is important with every club from driver to putter.

Correcting the aim will eliminate compensations. The brain is really smart. If they misaim, the brain will say, "Hey partner, we are aimed to the right. Guess we have to come over the top and pull it left." They will find a way to compensate by maneuvering the putter or club and their swing in a way that creates results no matter what it looks or feels like. People are great learners.

Helpful hints for successful putting:
- Be sure that the eyes are over the ball or slightly inside.
- Control the putter with the dominant hand and a light hold.
- The putter should be flat on the ground for best results. (Adjust stance or bend putter if necessary.)
- Hands should be facing each other with thumbs down the center of the shaft.
- The putter shaft should be positioned up the inside of the left leg for right-handed people.
- The body should be standing tall with a slight bend at the knees and hips. Hands and arms should be hanging from the shoulders.
- Make a pendulum swing the same distance back and through depending on the distance. The putter stays on the target line.
- Feeling how hard to hit the ball for distance comes with practice.
- Hold the putter face square to the target until the ball drops into the hole.
- Usually greens slope toward water and away from mountains.
- Students should also learn about the grain (the direction grass grows) on the putting surface, and know that the ball moves faster with the grain and slower against the grain. Grass bends toward the setting sun and its direction can usually be detected by walking up to the hole and carefully looking at the edges.
- The ball also takes the break more during the last part of the putt as it slows down. It is important to notice the three feet around the hole.

Some helpful hints about putting practice:
- Putt every third putt with your eyes closed to increase feeling.
- Practice making putts instead of missing putts.
- If, in practice, you start missing putts get closer to the hole until you are making them, and then move back.
- Practice with one ball to different targets as golf is played.
- Putt your brains out. It is 43% of your score.
- Think you are a good putter or fake it until you make it.
- Use Chuck Hogan's In-sighter to check your aim or send for his Video, "Aim to Win" from Sports Enhancement by calling 800-345-4245, or at ChuckHogan.com.

Something to Think About

How do you know where you are going, if you don't have a plan and a target? Is it just out there somewhere? Do you just hit and hope? What do you think quarterbacks, basketball players, hockey players and archers think about and focus on?

BALL FLIGHT LAWS

If you know the ball flight laws, you can be your own coach. Learn them and use them to work the ball high and low, right and left. Experiment with the different ways to manipulate the flight of the ball, its initial direction and its eventual outcome. The ball will always start in the direction the club swings and the ball will always curve in the direction the club faces at impact. Study the picture below. There are only nine ways a ball can go.

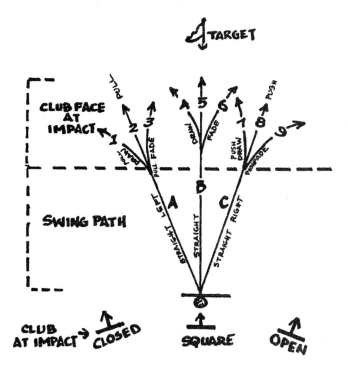

A. Swing path left of target

	Pull
1. Clubface closed at impact	Draw or hook
2. Clubface square at impact	Straight left
3. Club open at impact	Fade – slice

B. Swing path square to target

4. Clubface closed at impact	Hook or draw
5. Clubface square at impact	Straight
6. Clubface open at impact	Slice or fade

C. Swing path right of target

	Push
7. Clubface closed at impact	Hook or draw
8. Clubface square at impact	Straight right
9. Clubface open at impact	Slice or fade

There are other factors influencing the flight of the ball including lie angle and shaft specifics. The lie angle is one of the most important factors and can be easily tested with a lie board. I won't go into much more detail about club design and its effects except to attach the following drawing. Every teacher or coach needs to have some knowledge of these principles.

Having clubs fit your swing is just as important as having a perfect tennis racket, skis with sharp edges or a football that is correctly inflated. Club fitting is best done by an experienced teacher-club fitter, however, knowing the basics is helpful in teaching and coaching. Every golfer should be fit for clubs from the beginning. The Henry Griffiths Club Fitting technique is a great method. There are many qualified Henry Griffiths Club Fitters all over the nation. You can find one in your area by calling 1-800-445-4653.

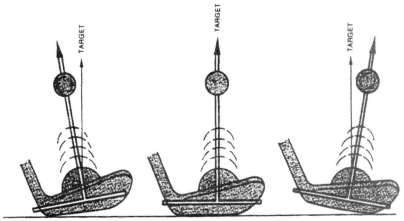

LIE TOO UPRIGHT   **CORRECT LIE**   **LIE TOO FLAT**

BALL WILL BE HIT   STRAIGHT SHOT   BALL WILL BE HIT
LEFT OF TARGET   RIGHT OF TARGET

NOTE: Even though the leading edge of the club is perpendicular to the desired direction of flight, the plane on the face of either a too upright or too flat lie club will hit the ball either left or right of the target respectively.

Fig. 59-4
Improper lie can cause directional problems

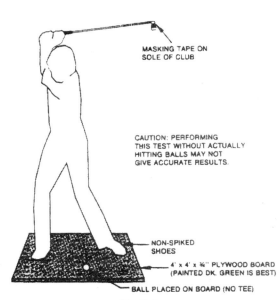

MASKING TAPE ON
SOLE OF CLUB

CAUTION: PERFORMING
THIS TEST WITHOUT ACTUALLY
HITTING BALLS MAY NOT
GIVE ACCURATE RESULTS.

NON-SPIKED
SHOES

4' x 4' x ¾" PLYWOOD BOARD
(PAINTED DK. GREEN IS BEST)

BALL PLACED ON BOARD (NO TEE)

Fig. 59-5
Checking for proper lie angle

From Roger Maltby's book *Golf Club Design....*

173

Something to Think About

Have clubs fit to your swing instead of fitting your swing to the clubs.

YARDAGE BOOKS

Yardage books were non-existent in the old days. Golfers played by the seat of their pants so to speak. They played by intuition or they guessed. They just hit it and either found it and hit it again or did not find it and dropped another ball. Golf has gotten more complicated since then. Course architects have included hazards and subtle variations that are not visible from far away. So, knowing the course or having information ahead of time has become more important. Professionals know how far a target is within a few feet. In tournament play, we play a practice round to get more information. Yardage books are used to plan our attack and remind us of the game plan for each hole. In college, we play the same courses many times during the years of eligibility of each student, yardage books are a good reminder of how we did in the past and how, if necessary, we can do things better. Here is an example of a page in a yardage book. There are many different ways to keep the information about each hole, some more detailed than others are.

Drawing a hole for your notebook:

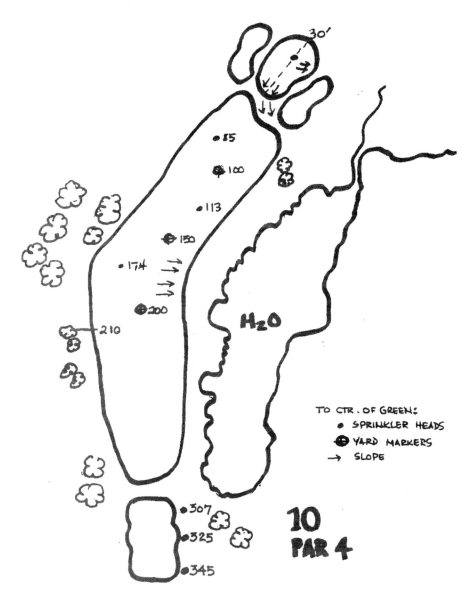

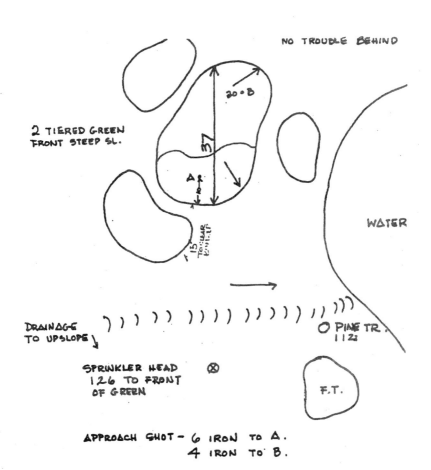

NO TROUBLE BEHIND

20 • B

2 TIERED GREEN
FRONT STEEP SL.

37

A
B

WATER

15
TO REAR
R. H. UP

DRAINAGE
TO UPSLOPE

O PINE TR.
1 12:

SPRINKLER HEAD   ⊗
126 TO FRONT
OF GREEN

F.T.

APPROACH SHOT - 6 IRON TO A.
4 IRON TO B.

DRIVE CENTER- R

USE 3 WOOD SO WON'T BE ON DN. SLOPE.
FAIRWAY SLOPES TO H₂0

#1

O   •   •   336   4 PAR
PINE TREE

MORE ABOUT PLAYING A HOLE

On the tee:
1. Open up the view of the fairway by playing from the right or left side of the tee.
2. Know that the tee markers do not always point you in the right direction.
3. Plan for the second shot.
4. If you have a chance play an iron, like a 5 iron, twice for a par 4 or three times for a par 5 to see where the best place is to land your shots. Sometimes 15 right or left feet makes a big difference.
5. What if you didn't hit your shot quite where you intended? Where is the best place to miss it if that happens? Plan for this.

From the fairway:
1. Never let your emotions dictate your decision.
2. Walk the hole backwards from the opening of the green. You will get a clearer picture of where you want to be in order to have a clear shot to the pin. You will be surprised at the difference you feel when you have a clear shot as opposed to having to cross the corner of a bunker for example.
3. Many times, it is better to hit a longer club if you have to go over trouble even if it means a downhill putt. It is better than possibly missing your shot short into the trouble and then having to take an extra shot. Does that make sense?
4. Never aim at trouble.
5. Know the distance to clear the trouble if necessary, including bunkers.

IDEAS FOR IMPROVING YOUR GAME

1. Play 18 holes with three clubs. You can pick any three clubs. See if your score changes much.
2. Play from the red, white or blue tee changing from day to day.
3. Walk the course backwards for a new perspective.
4. Play 18 holes with no pins on the green. What will that change?
5. Play a round and on each hole, when you reach the green, throw the ball in one of the bunkers and count from there.
6. Play mulligan golf. Once in your head and once for real. Grade your mulligan on a scale of 1 to 10 as to how vivid it was.
7. Play counting from 100 yards in.
8. Play evaluating your attitude on each shot. Scale 1 to 10, ten being best.
9. Play 100% golf. Grade your participation on each shot on a scale from 1 to 10.
10. Play counting putts only for the putting championship.
11. Play for a chance to participate in the US Open.
12. Play pretending you are Tiger Woods or Annika Sorenstam or your favorite player.
13. Play each shot and evaluate the amount of fun it was. Scale 1 to 10.

PLAY

Play, jump in puddles, hop over barriers, do somersaults in the fairway, aim at the bunker or water, play backwards, play left handed, talk to the squirrels, stick flowers in your hair, lay down and get up, yell "hooray" after a good shot, sing a song, say hello to the workers, feel up, feel down, feel happy, walk backwards, throw grass in wind, hug you partner, smile at the trees, be silly, have fun, celebrate just being there. Use your imagination.

Something to Think About

You can never have too much fun. It would be like having too much money.

TEN REASONS WHY PEOPLE WHO WORK VERY HARD ON THEIR GOLF GAME AREN'T AS SUCCESSFUL AS THEY SHOULD BE

1. Not focused
2. Not efficient.
3. Too many distractions.
4. Bad habits.
5. Poor instruction or coaching or too much instruction or too many instructors.
6. Goals and priorities are not clear.
7. Equipment is not right.
8. Time management problem.
9. Their thinking is counter-productive
10. Poor health, physical fitness or diet problems.

Something to Think About

"I love competitions so much that when I'm alone, I compete with myself. Shooting baskets or playing golf or whatever I do, I pretend that I'm someone else. I take my shots, then take the opposition's shots. I've always been that way. I play hard against myself."

Bruce Lietzke

Note: Have a passion for what you do whatever it is. Play and practice for the love of it. Make competition fun. It is a choice you are able to make.

WAYS TO ASSIST YOUR PLAYERS AT TOURNAMENTS
Or ways to be successful playing the game.

These suggestions may give you ideas to help your players.

1. Play the round in your mind the night before. Find a quiet place and with your eyes closed imagine playing each hole. This exercise actually can give you an extra practice round.

2. Make a list of 10 things you do well and read them on the way to the golf course.

3. Dance only to your music by listening to music that fits your swing on the way to the course. You could have your own recorder to listen to five songs that fit your swing. It is a mistake to get into somebody else's rhythm.

4. Get to the course one hour ahead of tee time leaving enough time for personal things so that there is no rushing.

5. Leave all problems on the seat of the van or car. They will be there when you return.

6. Warm up the body and the mind on the practice area. Do not work on mechanics or attempt to change your swing. The purpose of warming up is to discover how you are swinging for that day. Changes can be made after the round or after the tournament.

7. Be sure you leave enough time to get the feel of the putting green. The important part here is to get the feeling for distance. By taking out the element of the hole and putting to the edges of the green isolates distance response.

8. Maybe it would be a good idea if you putted first, then hit

balls on the range making your last shot a good one with the club you are going to hit on the first tee.

9. You should think of yourself as bigger, brighter and more colorful than anyone else and the best player on the course.

10. You can decide to feel confident, peaceful and patient.

11. You can ask for what you want. I want to putt well today. Instead of I am not putting well today. You **will** get what you ask for.

12. You can commit to walking, talking and acting like a winner no matter what happens. You can continue this body language throughout the round. A good idea might be to think about your favorite golfer and act, as he/she would act.

13. You can make a choice to think only about golf during the round.

14. You could think of walking down a tunnel, through a brightly colored door or down a red carpet to the first tee feeling self-assured and surrendering to your swing for that day and playing just do it golf.

15. Make everything and everybody that day a collaborator in your success guiding you to the target.

16. Make a good yardage book during the practice round keeping a record of clubs hit to the different targets.

17. Have a game plan and stick to it.

18. Stay in the present. Forget the past and do not worry about the future.

19. Commit to giving every shot 100%. Do the best you can on each shot, one shot at a time.

20. Smile, understanding that you make yourself happy by doing so.

21. Anchor your good shots. (See chapter on anchoring.)

22. Be positive about everything. Negativity will kill your game and getting serious will retard your imagination.

23. Be totally target-oriented for the entire round.

24. You must stick to your preshot routine on EVERY shot.

25. Be courteous, respectful and polite to playing partners, spectators and officials.

26. Pull the flag if you are the closest to the pin after marking your ball, and replace pin if you are the first to putt out.

27. Repair ball marks on the green.

28. Make a choice not to get upset with slower players ahead of their group or in their group, and with other people's behavior. What they resist persists.

29. Keeping up with the group ahead is more important than concentrating on the people behind.

30. Play as if the course was your favorite course, favorite hole, favorite weather and favorite playing partners.

31. Praise your partner's good shots.

32. Wave to or signal your teammates when you see them. It creates team spirit.

33. Know the rules and follow them.

34. Take rules advice only from rules officials.

35. Pretend you are having fun if not everything is going your way.

36. Think of how lucky you are to be playing golf.

37. Give them only two seconds to talk about bad shots after the round.

38. After the round, talk about the shot of the day or the hole of the day or the putt of the day. Give each person a turn.

39. Cool down after the round by hitting a few shots and working on the short game.

40. Rest and prepare the mind and body for the next round.

Playing golf is easy. [14]
- Warm up your body and mind.
- Make a decision. (What do you want?)
- Hit the ball.
- Anchor the good.
- Chase the ball.

---

[14] Chuck Hogan

- Gather information for the next shot
- Make a decision.
- Hit the ball.
- Fall in love with the shot.
- Play.
- Replay the good.
- Enjoy yourself.

Final advice to players before the tournament:

Enjoy the tournament. Act, walk and talk like champions. Win or lose, you are the best. Give 100%, do the best you possibly can, play to win, but no matter what happens, learn to love the experience.

Extras

During an important tournament, there are extras that you can do to create a winning atmosphere. I remember at one national championship showing the team the movie *Angels in the Outfield*, a baseball movie. As a result, whenever they made a good shot, they waved both arms like they were flying. That feeling of joy they saw and heard in the movie lasted the whole tournament.

Also, I can recall giving everyone a water gun on a very hot practice round at a national championship to use when anyone got serious. The feeling of fun lasted the whole tournament.

The right movies are a great way to relax and capture the exhilarated feelings of joy. Sometimes movies can put life and golf or sports in perspective.

The following is a partial list of movies you could use with teams or individuals to create an atmosphere of joy, inspiration and spirit.

- *Chariots of Fire*
- *Fly Away Home*
- *Angels in the Outfield*
- *Field of Dreams*
- *Forrest Gump*
- *Hoosiers*
- *Lorenzo's Oil*
- *The Horse Whisperer*
- *Rudy*
- *Patch Adams*
- *Nell*

CHAPTER VI

Aspects of Highly Effective
Teams and Individuals

THE IMPORTANCE OF GETTING FIT FOR CLUBS

Having clubs that fit your swing and reward your motions is essential. It is important right from the beginning of the learning process. However many golfers are guilty of playing golf with clubs that do not fit them. When they make mistakes, they always think it is their fault. They do not understand how clubs can affect their swings, and the resulting direction and distance of the ball flight. This is also true of coaches, teachers and especially some club fitters.

Getting fitted is essential, if someone wants to learn to play golf efficiently. Beginners and children just starting the learning process should have two or three fitted clubs. With non-fitting clubs, it is a survival test on the golf course. They learn to use the equipment and survive with compensating and complicated swings. Once learners or experienced golfers have the correct equipment, they can make a choice to change the compensations or learn the correct motions. However, either way, if you have incorrect clubs, you will have to compensate differently using the short irons and long irons. Learners are never going to have one swing that is going to hold up throughout with one set of clubs. Having clubs that fit each golfer's swing will minimize the compensations; and allow the golfer to make a swing that works for all the clubs.

Clubs do make you swing a certain way, but that goes hand and hand with understanding the golf swing. Therefore, it is not always the equipment. That is where the **teacher-fitter** is important. The teacher-fitter can decipher if it is actually the equipment or the person's motion. The bottom line is always that the student is going to swing the way he is rewarded.

ANCHORING

Anchoring is a physical motion performed after doing something good, or bad in your opinion. (*i.e.* a good shot, a great speech, a bet won.) An example of anchoring is Tiger Woods pumping his fist. Or a smile you make after you solve a problem and you think, "Yep, I did it." It does not have to be extreme. It could be just touching your nose, clapping your hands, your thumb in the air or even that smile, but it must be something physical. You must get emotionally attached to it. If you hit a bad shot in your opinion, it does not mean that you should not recognize it as a bad shot. It means that you do not attach emotion to it and make it a painful experience.

I bet that you have watched many people anchor their bad shots. You see it all the time on the golf course, on the range and putting green. People hit themselves, throw clubs, pound the ground, hit trees, punch their fist thru a wall, etc. etc. Think of anchoring as building a library in your brain. It is important to build a library of good shots and good experiences. Then when you are about to hit a shot, or accomplish a particular task and you can recall one that is similar from your library, it is like hitting a mulligan or having a dress rehearsal. Would you like to play a round of golf with a mulligan on every shot? How do you think you would you play? Why in the world would anyone want to build a library of bad experiences? If your entire library held bad experiences, how do you think you would do? Think about it.

Some people think that getting things off their chest is a positive action. Maybe they associate it with a feeling of relief. Think about the energy it takes to get mad and pound the ground. It is such a negative way to react. Could you use that energy in a more positive way? Certainly, if we use positive ways to express ourselves, it is much more rewarding.

It is what you do after hitting a shot that counts.

To play your best golf, you have to do the following:

- Anchor your good shots. Get excited with the things you do right.
- Anchors need to be timed just as the state of mind is reaching its peak.
- Anchors must be unique and distinctive.
- Easy to repeat.
- Something associated with your senses.
- Build a library of good shots in your brain by being emotionally attached to the good things that you do. You will be able to recall them later.

Examples:

- Pump your fist *a la* Tiger Woods.
- Run around the green *a la* Hale Irwin.
- Thumbs up.
- Smile or smile inwardly.
- Say YES out loud.
- Touch your ear.
- Tap your side.
- Hug your caddie.
- Give a high five. *Etc.*

Something to Think About

A team can accomplish remarkable things if nobody cares who gets the credit.

THE DAY OF PLAY[15]

SLOW DOWN A BIT.
SEE YOURSELF MAKING GOOD SHOTS.
FEEL THE FEELINGS, HEAR THE MAXIMS.
DEPOSIT ANY DISTRACTIONS IN THE VAN ON YOUR SEAT.
IMAGINE POURING INTO YOUR BODY A WARM, FLUID, QUIET
    SENSE OF CONFIDENCE, PATIENCE AND ESTEEM.
FROM THIS POINT ON.... WALK, TALK, THINK LIKE A CHAMPION NO
    MATTER WHAT HAPPENS, CONTINUE THE BODY LANGUAGE.
ASSUME THIS POSTURE THAT MAKES YOU FEEL STRONG, AND
    CONFIDENT.
STAND TALLER.
TAKE ON THE PHYSICAL CHARACTERISTICS OF A CHAMPION
    WHATEVER THAT MEANS TO YOU.
MAKE EVERY PERSON OR OBJECT YOUR ALLY IN GREAT GOLF.
    IMAGINE THAT EVERYTHING ON THE GOLF COURSE IS THERE
    TO DEFINE AND CONTRIBUTE TO YOUR SHOTS. EVERYTHING
    ON THE COURSE IS THERE TO GUIDE YOU TO THE TARGET.
WALK DOWN THE TUNNEL TO THE FIRST HOLE SURRENDERING TO
    THE SWING YOU HAVE FOR THAT DAY AND PLAY NIKE GOLF.
    JUST DO IT. THE MOTOR IS WARMED UP AND WORKING. BE
    CONFIDENT THAT IT WILL GET YOU THERE.

PLAYING GOLF IS EASY.
    WARM UP YOUR BODY AND MIND.
    MAKE A DECISION. (WHAT DO YOU WANT?)
    HIT THE BALL.
    ANCHOR THE GOOD.
    CHASE THE BALL.
    GATHER INFORMATION FOR THE NEXT SHOT.
    MAKE A DECISION.
    HIT THE BALL.
    FALL IN LOVE WITH THE SHOT.
    PLAY.
    REPLAY THE GOOD.
    ENJOY YOURSELF.

HAVE A GREAT TIME OR A TIME THAT IS GREAT.

---

[15] Chuck Hogan.

UP AND DOWN

Athletes have often remarked to me, when they make a mistake, about feeling down and having the tendency to make more mistakes. I remember, Kay Cockerill in her first year at UCLA saying to me during a tournament round, "I'm on a bogie train, Coach, how do I get off?" Then again, there were times when she was up, confident and successful in everything she did. This syndrome is what Chuck Hogan calls the spiral effect, which is illustrated on the following pages.

Whenever one is playing golf, frustration can set in. Your feelings can take you down to the very depths of your emotions or you can do something different, make a different choice and take the opposite journey to euphoria. In the downward spiral your swing can deteriorate, your shots can get worse, your demeanor can change and you get angry and depressed. It's not fun anymore. However, by choice, you can change the situation, do something different, reverse the spiral effect, and go the other way. You can choose to become interested and want to take part. You can decide to be ready, trusting and believing. These kinds of choices will put you in the upward spiral and will allow you to achieve the zone and euphoria you are always looking for. It's a happy time. When you do become aware that you are frustrated, it is time to do something different, anything different. Do a cartwheel. Walk backwards. Think different. Change your opinion. Pretend. You will be pleasantly surprised.

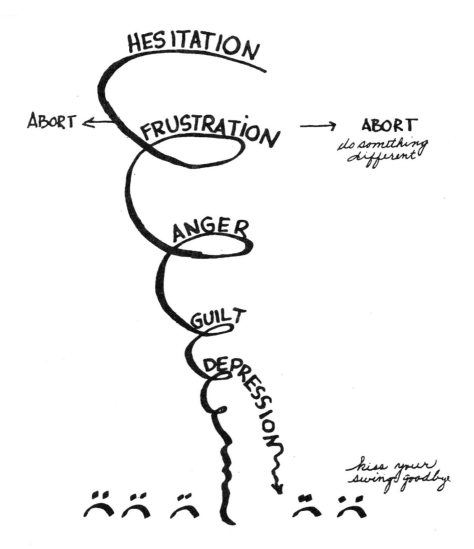

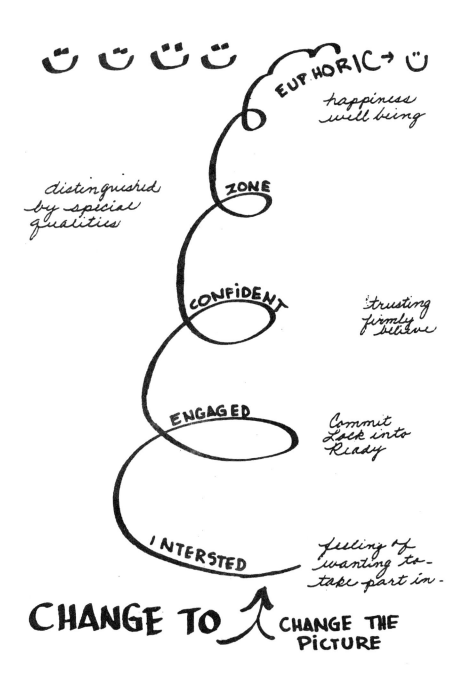

EUPHORIC → ☺
*happiness
will being*

*distinguished
by special
qualities*

ZONE

CONFIDENT

*trusting
firmly
believe*

ENGAGED

*Commit
Lock into
Ready*

INTERSTED

*feeling of
wanting to-
take part in -*

CHANGE TO ↟ CHANGE THE PICTURE

WHAT DOES A COACH, TEACHER OR PARENT SAY AND DO AFTER A TOURNAMENT ROUND?

This is a touchy period. Feelings, attitudes and emotions are involved. How they played is a big part of this after-the-round time period. No matter what you do or say, you cannot please everybody. You must be yourself. You must be honest, sympathetic and nurturing. You must act from your heart. It is difficult to know what to do or say sometimes. You have a right to be excited, discouraged or disappointed just like anybody else, but if they win or lose, there must be unconditional acceptance. Raving, ranting, or punishing is unacceptable behavior for coaches, teachers and parents. What you do will influence them now or later. You are the model.

After a cooling off period, you can do several things. Start with a positive note. Praise them first for what they did well with true honesty and compassion. Have them talk about their round or you can start by asking a question.

Examples:
- What are the good shots you made today?
- On reflection, what could you have done better?
- Look at the statistics. What does that tell you?
- What would you do differently next time? .
- What specifically do you need to practice?
- Would you play any hole differently?
- Did you do your best on every shot?
- Did you maintain a good attitude the whole round?
- Did you talk nice to yourself?
- Did you give yourself credit?
- Did you anchor your good shots?

- Were you patient?
- What were your goals today? Did you accomplish them?

Let them become aware of what is working and not working. If they have nothing to say, ask them to guess or pretend they know, or ask what if questions. What if you did...?

DREAMS

Dreams are what success is all about. All successful coaches have dreams, and thus are winners. I doubt that success comes without dreams and a passion to go after them. So how do and, more importantly, why do coaches become winners? They become winners, because their goals, their dreams, have defined what they truly want. They recruit talented players who have the same attributes. When the coach and the athletes are going in the same direction and working to achieve the same things, then success is a forgone conclusion.

Players who dream big and want to be winners are more likely to accomplish their goals because they will find a way to win, do whatever it takes, and have the determination to succeed. They overlook the small stuff, eliminate distractions, and minimize anything that gets in their way. They go after what they want hook, line and sinker.

Being successful, winning and achieving greatness takes patience and persistence as well as many disappointments and frustrations in the process, but the process is the important part and with enough determination along the way to get better and better, the rewards will be evident. Coaches with this attitude will be the ones at the top on whatever scale they choose. We coach because we have a chance to realize our dreams and assist others in reaching theirs.

Something to Think About

"The thing about dreams is sometimes you get to live them out."

Payne Stewart

A LESSON ON DREAMS

A person with great dreams can achieve great things. What are your dreams? What do you want? Please list below. What are you willing to do every day to accomplish these goals? Please send me a copy and post a copy on your bathroom mirror or bedroom door so that you will see it **every single day.**

Here is a very good plan: Every night before you go to sleep, think about and dream "what it would be like to win the National Championship this year." What would it feel like? Can you picture in your mind coming off the 18th green knowing you won the Nationals? Can you picture the team? What would they be doing? Can you picture the reactions of all of us? Can you imagine walking up to receive the trophy? Can you picture the first time you put on your championship ring? You can do this. Do it every night. Put a note on your pillow to remind yourself to dream this dream before you go to sleep. Replace it every morning. A person with great dreams can, achieve great things.

A person with great dreams can achieve great things.

(You may have heard this before, but it is important that you hear it again and again.)

I recruited you all because I believed that somewhere inside, you had a <u>passion</u> for the game of golf. That you were totally committed to winning a National Championship in your years at UCLA. <u>I believe that this is that year</u>. That truly you are ready and willing to be the best that you can be. I believe that you are the most outstanding team ever in UCLA history, and in fact the best in the country and will demonstrate this fact at the end of the year.

I believe that you are committed to work on your pitching, chipping and putting until you become <u>absolutely excellent</u> at it, because <u>that's what makes a championship team</u>. I will bet you that most golfers in college spend most of their time on the range working on their swings and not many are around the practice green working on their short game. This takes discipline. <u>Success depends on this discipline as well as a player's attitude, how well she plays the wedges and the putter and how well she thinks</u>. You have that capability, you have that power, you have that attitude. It <u>is</u> your choice.

I believe that you can wake up every morning and yell "yippy skippy". I got to play golf today. I believe that you are able to look forward to each day because there is another opportunity to chase your dreams and smile at the end of the day knowing that you took one more step in accomplishing them. With this kind of attitude and determination, you could move mountains. You can!

The process not the result enriches your golf and your life. When you look back on this school year, I hope that you will look back with fond memories and realize that in your heart you chased your dreams with all that you had. <u>You have that opportunity, now</u>.

My best wishes for a very happy and successful New Year.

Love,
Coach

Something to Think About

Great athletes and coaches set their goals on something they believe, and refuse to give up until that dream is realized.

WANT
(EN)-VISION

BELIEFS
(EXPERIENCES, LEARNING)

BEHAVIOR
(ACTIONS, THINGS YOU ACTUALLY DO)

**MUST BE CONGRUENT WITH NO AMBIGUITY
POTENTIAL MINUS INTERFERENCE = PERFORMANCE**

CREATE WHAT YOU WANT

You can play successful golf or do and be anything you want if you really put your mind to it. It could start at this very minute. Here is how it works. Decide. Make a choice right now that your future will be something very special. Decide now that you could be a great golfer or special in any area of your life. The possibility of greatness is in your hands. What if you decided today is the day I start believing this? It can happen. Gifted athletes and successful people in all areas of life have the ability to put themselves in the future. They can determine what they would like to happen in the next week, year, or decade. The secret is getting the feelings of success before it happens. What would it feel like or make sense to you to be successful, to be a great player, a fantastic lawyer, a successful coach or even have a perfect golf shot or hit a home run? Set yourself up. Creating in your mind and stretching your imagination can make it happen.

Antidote: What you think about comes about.

BE CAREFUL WHAT YOU ASK FOR....
YOU'LL GET IT....

THE BRAIN DOESN'T CARE, IT WILL LEARN ANYTHING.

ASK FOR WHAT YOU WANT....
DON'T ASK FOR ANYTHING ELSE....
GREAT CONCEPT....
IT ISN'T WHAT YOU SAY....
WHAT YOU THINK IS WHAT YOU GET....

WE ARE ALWAYS ASKING—
        I GOTTA GO TO CLASS...
        I ALWAYS MISS SHORT PUTTS...
        I CAN'T PUTT TODAY...
        MY DRIVER ISN'T WORKING...
        I CAN'T SEEM TO PICK THE RIGHT CLUB...
        THIS IS NOT MY DAY...
        I TRY SO HARD AND IT STILL DOESN'T WORK...

GET INTO YOUR SENSES, FIND THE FEELING, MAKE A CHOICE...
IT MUST BE CLEAR
IT IS THE BASIS FOR YOUR POTENTIAL...
THINKING IS A BLEND OF SMELL FEEL SEE HEAR TASTE
OTHERWISE YOU WILL HAVE CONFUSION AND AMBIGUITY.
ANALYZING KEEPS US IN A TRYING MODE INSTEAD OF A
LETTING MODE....

TEAM VISIONING

1. Where are we now?
2. What do we do really well?
3. What do we not do well?
4. How are we perceived by other teams?
5. How are we perceived by individual members of this team?
6. What new demands will be placed on us the rest of the year?
   By the school?
   By the coach?
   By individual members of the team?
7. From who or what can we learn?
8. What should we improve?
9. How can we improve?
10. What part should each individual play? Should we change something?
11. How should we progress?
12. When should we review our progress?

GOALS

A great deal has been written about goals, how to set them and their purpose. Certainly, a goal is an important motivator. Goals are set everyday, every minute by everybody. If you do not have a map or a plan, how do you know where you are going? Good question!

Having a dream or a vision of what you want in your life is behind every successful athlete and coach. Your dreams and your belief that someday you can accomplish those dreams are what start the process and keep you going. Becoming your dream, being your vision, is what commitment is all about. These are the choices you make. As you set your goals and dream your dreams, go one step at a time. You will gain momentum, get stronger and benefit more by doing the best you possibly can every minute of every day. Whatever you choose to do in your life or in sports, you will be rewarded by your choice of actions. What you do today affects tomorrow. Yesterday is history.

In golf and in other sports, we are all moving in a direction. So some of us are going forward, some of us are going backwards and some of us are going in the direction of whatever the golf magazines and TV commentators or advertisers tell us to go. It is a known fact that we get what we ask for. Wouldn't it be a good idea to ask for what you want? Successful people ask the right questions and then they focus on what they want, and, in the process, firmly believe that they can accomplish it. Look at it like this. What you want, what you believe and what you do all have to be working together. You cannot have one without the other if you want to be successful. So if you watch one of your athletes always hitting balls on the driving range but saying she wants to be the best short game player in the country, there is something wrong. What does she really want?

Let me tell you a little story. I recruited a young lady in her senior year of high school who told me she wanted to be the best putter in college golf. That really impressed me. She definitely had a worthwhile goal and one that would take her a long way in competitive golf. Of course, knowing that putting is 40% of your score, it was an intelligent goal. Eunice is intelligent, attended UCLA and did become the best putter in college golf, the top of the heap for two years. It was a real success story and an example of commitment to what she wanted.

So, take look at your behavior and the behavior of those you advise and instruct, and you can tell what they **really** want. Guide yourself and your athletes in discovering exactly where they want to go and exactly how to get there, and more importantly, let them discover the enjoyment along the way. Each step in your journey will bring you joy.

So now, let us look at goals and how you can teach athletes to achieve what they want.

GOALS:

1. Goals must be in writing.
2. Long range goals and dreams do not necessarily have to be realistic in the beginning.
3. Goals must be reviewed often.
4. Goals must be something people desperately want.
5. They must be each individual's desire, not someone else's. A team goal must be agreed on by all members of the team.
6. Individuals must succeed at short-term goals on a daily basis in order to reach their intermediate and long term goals and ultimately their dream.

You can be or achieve anything you want, if you are willing to believe it can be done, and you are willing to commit to what it takes to get you there. One just has to look at people like Tara Lapinski, Michael Jordan, Wayne Gretzky, Tiger Woods and Michelle Kwan to just name a few. Athletes, and you as a coach, must have a vision and then commit to becoming that vision.

Stretch your goals, dream big dreams and follow what makes you happy.

The following are some examples of drawings and forms that can assist you in teaching goals. There are many ways to accomplish this lesson. Use your imagination. A dream is a dream. It is something that you want to happen someday.

Your goals are specific. They are actions and results of what you want. You must have a way to measure them. You must believe that you can achieve them and they must be realistic. Goals are handled on a day-to-day, week-to-week, and month-to-month basis.

You are 100% responsible for the results in your life, on some level, otherwise, your life would be different.

SOME WAYS TO START LESSONS ON GOALS

GOALS 1996

I WANT TO WIN THE NCAA'S WITH MY TEAM AND INDIVIDUAL

FOR THAT I WILL WORK HARD ON MY GAME BY:
SPENDING TIME ON THE PUTTING GREENS SO THAT I WILL HAVE NO DOUBTS

WORK ON MY ATTITUDE BY:
RELAXING ON COURSE CONCENTRATE ONLY ON GOOD SHOTS AND HANDLE POOR SHOTS WITH NO EMOTION

THINKING ABOUT GOOD THINGS THAT HAVE HAPPENED IN THE PAST AND WILL HAPPEN AGAIN AND AGAIN
I WILL WORK OUT AND RUN AS MUCH AS I CAN SO THAT I CAN BECOME STRONGER AND BE THE BEST THAT I CAN BE

What are your dreams??

What do you want???

UCLA

NCAA

Champions

1991

Please post on your door at school and at home so you see every day.

Where do I go from here?

- What do I want?
- How can I get there?
- What do I need to give up?
- What specific things do I need to do to make sure I will give myself the best opportunity to succeed?

The warmth of the sun is shining upon the UCLA team as we watch the last scores being posted on the board. Our eyes light up with happiness as we realize that we've won the ASU tournament by five shots. Coach is beaming with excitement and her smile looks a mile wide.

LINDA VOLLSTEDT begins the awards ceremony and we wait in anticipation to accept our trophy. Linda finally says the magic words, "the winning team, UCLA." We all go to the front and accept our sweet reward. As we stand infront of the crowd our hearts fill with a soft fuzzy feeling and we all realize that this is just the beggining.

MY GOALS AND DREAMS

Below are real samples of students' goals:

Player #1

- To have a lower scoring average than last year

- Win a collegiate tournament

- Become an All-American

- Have a team and individual NCAA title

- Be under par in a collegiate tournament

- Win the US Women's Amateur

- Play on the LPGA tour and travel around the world

Player #2

- Decrease my scoring average to 72

- Increase National Rank to top 10

- Think success every time I hit the ball

- Be more up

- Hit 13 greens in regulation or better

- Average 28 putts per round

- Think every chip in the hole

- Pitch to within 6 feet

Player #3

- **Win NCAA Golf Championship team and individual**

- **Be LPGA Rookie of the Year**

- **Be LPGA Player of the Year**

- **Be in the LPGA Hall of Fame in 10 years**

- **Have a great marriage and my own family who always will love each other**

- **Pursue my academic research after golf**

- **Always put my best effort into everything that I do**

- **Mentally practice being there every day and achieving my dreams**

- **Physically practice golf**

- **Work out regularly to be physically fit**

- **Every time I take on a task, I will give my best effort, one task at a time**

- **Keep up my academic interests even after graduation**

Something to Think About

With enough dreams and the commitment to achieve them, the golf game can be turned into a piece of art.

HOW COULD YOU PRACTICE WINNING?

(A WAY TO PRESENT A LESSON)

Agenda

- **Goals for the rest of the year.**
- **What am I willing to give up?**
- **What is trusting and how can we learn to trust?**
- **How can we practice winning?**
- **Where do you want to be in May?**
- **How are you going to get there?**

We are getting to the end of the season.

April 1, 1998

Hello !

Rules

- No idea is a bad idea
- Be creative
- Take risks
- No criticism allowed

TRUST

■ Trust is a feeling. It is a sense. It is connection with the target. It is being the target. It is the circle from you to the target and back again. It is a state of mind. It is being present. It is a firm belief. It is faith. It is the power of a person. It is confidence. It is commitment, It is your belief.

What is playing this week in your movie?

■There is a movie in my mind, and it has a happy ending.

Tara Lapinski

■ "I practiced winning."

■ When I was a little girl my father built stands for the winners—first, second and third. I always climbed to the top one and pretended I won the Olympic Games.

WHAT A CONCEPT!

Something to Think About

Here is a great example of clever insight by Ted Oh, professional golfer and former UCLA player. One day, during a meeting with one of my athletes about her lack of commitment, she told me about some advice made by her brother. This is what he said. "Julie, you just got a new car, yes? What if you had to take your car into the shop, because it was always breaking down? How would you feel?" Julie's answer, "I would be very disappointed." Then Ted said, "How do you think Coach Steinmann feels?"

Something to Think About

This team is not going to be as good as I want it to be,
but it is going to be as good as you want it to be.

TRUST AND COMMITMENT

If you say you are going to do something and you do it, you become more trustworthy. When people trust you, you create respect. Do what you say you are going to do. It is true that making a commitment just to be on time is as important as being honest. Keeping your commitments is essential to trust. Naturally, we all slip a little at times, but making the effort to be trustworthy will pay off in golf, life, relationships business and **coaching**.

TRUST

Trust is a firm belief, truthfulness, justice, and power of a person, faith, and confident expectation or hope. The ability to trust comes from our experiences. If we only understand what we are doing, which by the way is the booby prize, and we don't feel it in our bodies, we can't really trust. We know how to do many things for example in our daily lives that we really don't think about. We just do them. We don't analyze them or control them consciously. If we don't do them right or make a mistake somehow, we do not worry about it, we just go on. Think about the things you do on a daily basis. You get out of bed, you brush your teeth, you eat breakfast, *etc.* Don't you trust yourself to do these things without thinking?

If you drop something on the floor, you don't go to the dropping range for a lesson on how to hold something in your hand. You trust that you can and will be able to hold something in your hand at any given time and you go on.

So when it comes to your golf swing, what do most people do? As soon as they make a mistake, they think it is something wrong with their swing and they go for a swing lesson.

You can only trust, if you can feel or sense what is happening. It has been said many times that golf is an easy game. Golf is an easy game. It is people who make it difficult. Moreover, definitely if you believe it is difficult it will be. If you don't sense what you are doing it will be difficult. In other words, if you can't feel what you are doing in your golf swing by experiencing and becoming aware of what you are doing, you will always think it is difficult. Making sense or non-sense of what you are doing is a crucial step in successful performance and trusting.

Let me give you an example. Let's take the putting stroke for example. What do you sense when you make a good putt? Do the following exercise as an experiment. Step up to your ball, after aiming, put your putter behind the ball, and then close your eyes and putt in the direction of the hole. With your eyes closed, determine by feel the direction the ball actually took. Then look at the results. Were you surprised? This is what becoming aware of your senses means. Learning to sense what you do creates trust. So let's look at some specific shots. What is it like to slice, fade, hook or draw the ball? What feeling do you get in your body when you want the ball to high or low? Someone can tell you how to do it, but it won't be effective until you feel what it takes to accomplish the task. If you don't look, how do you know what happened?

After you learn to pay attention to what you feel, you must trust your instincts. You felt it. Did it feel good or bad? Now you have a choice. Choose to feel what makes a good swing or shot and abandon the bad feelings. Stop wondering what you are doing wrong when you play. Instead, notice the feelings, the sense you get, and which sense works. Confidence and trust will build at an alarming rate. Stop doing the things that don't work. Stop the "what ifs." Change it. Learning and enjoyment are always under your control.

Trust comes from the sense you make of things. Experiencing is the way we learn. Change your images instead of changing your swing. Be guided by the feelings or the signals, you get. Trust and confidence go hand in hand.

- Trust in me as your coach.
- Trust in your fellow team members.
- Trust that your practice will pay off.
- Trust your swing.
- Trust in your putting stroke.
- Trust that you can reach your goals.

- Trust in your ability.
- Trust it and bust it.
- Trust it and let it happen.
- Trust it and give yourself a chance.
- Train so that you can trust.
- It is far better to always trust than to always train.
- Trust instincts and intuition. Look and react.

Something to Think About

Ambiguous: Doubtful, clouded, dubious, indecisive, precarious, problematic, queasy, shady, suspect, suspicious, uncertain, unclear, undecided, uneasy, unsettled, unstable, unsure, incongruent, iffy, hazy, obscure, unlikely. **If any of these are going on before or during a shot, you're done, cooked, finished.**

CHARACTERISTICS OF HIGHLY EFFECTIVE TEAMS

1. Players share a clear and shared vision of why the team exists.
2. Play is managed against clear, well-defined goals.
3. Priorities are understood and agreed to.
4. Processes are created to get things done efficiently.
5. Team unity contributes to good morale.
6. Individual autonomy and interdependence are in balance.
7. Little time is wasted.
8. Risk and failure are accepted and learned from.
9. Innovation and experimentation are encouraged.
10. Members believe in helping each other routinely.
11. Decision-making is mostly by consensus.
12. Problems are solved efficiently and effectively.
13. Team is task-focused and action-oriented.
14. Team members treat each other with integrity and dignity.
15. Individual role, talent and responsibility are well understood.
16. Member contributions are recognized and rewarded.
17. Team atmosphere is congenial and comfortable.
18. Power is shared.
19. Conflicts and differences are accepted, valued and confronted.
20. Leaders keep team focused, future-oriented and inspired.
21. Players have confidence in each other's commitment and ability.
22. People talk to each other clearly and frequently.
23. Timely and accurate feedback is sought.

24. People listen to each other for understanding.

25. Appropriate information is fully shared.

26. Communication processes are checked frequently.

27. Team sees itself as a unit with all people working together.

28. Team sees itself as unique and special.

29. Team and individual growth occurs.

30. The team has fun.

Adapted from Steven Covey.

GOOD-BAD NOTEBOOK

Are you or students aware of what you do when you play good or play bad? Would you like to learn to play good more often? How do you know you are in the zone? One way is to keep a good-bad notebook, a small one the size of your yardage book, in your golf bag. After every round of golf for about six weeks, if you play on a regular basis, write down on the left side of the notebook what you do when you play well and on the right side, what you do when you play badly. Keep your remarks as sensorial as possible, meaning try to relate them to your senses. What seems to make sense to you when you play good or bad. For example, today when I played I had a good rhythm, everything was perfectly clear. I felt strong, I felt like I was in a quite state. I was relaxed, everything was smooth. I walked with a confident walk. I smiled a lot. I did not get mad. I had fun. Start by listing as many things as you can about what you felt, saw and heard. Become aware of what worked for you on the course that day and what didn't work. When you did not hit a shot, what was it like? What were you thinking? Most likely your lists will be longer on the right, bad, side in the beginning. As you keep doing this, you will start to notice a pattern. Then all you have to do is stop the things on the right and keep doing the things on the left. Then how do you think you will play? Sound simple? It is simple, but it takes practice.

I found that when athletes started to become aware of the things they were doing, their attitude changed. They started to notice the things that got in their way. They got fascinated with the things that created good play. Now they could make some different choices. Remember the saying from NLP. If you always do what you've always done, you'll always get what you've always got. If what you are doing is not getting you what you want, do something different. Make a new choice.

This is very difficult to get people to do this exercise, even if it means that they will get better. Make them turn their notebooks in on a regular basis.

The whole crux of this exercise is to become aware of what you are thinking and doing, and then to make a choice.

Below is an example of an athlete's page in a good/bad notebook:

"Good"	"Bad"
Concentrate	Feel frustrated
Feel confident	Nothing is going right No matter what
Relaxed	Walking real slow
Having fun	Head down
See good outcomes of shots	Feel tired and lazy
Happy, patient	Swing feels lost
Feel everything going right	Not concentrating, mind in other places
Walking fast, smiling	feel like it's the slowest round of my Life
Putting great: see line of putt	Trying to play well to hard, searching for help
In touch with myself	Greens are hard to read
	Think about negative

It is vital to stop doing the things on the bad side if you are not getting you what

GOOD-BAD RESULTS

- Keep your good-bad notebook going continuously.
- Notice the patterns of the good and the bad.
- Keep saying "Isn't that fascinating" after you hit shots.
- Get fascinated with what you do.
- Get fascinated with how you play bad golf and then make a choice not to do that particular thing anymore.
- Get fascinated with how you play good golf and then make a choice to continue doing that particular think, whatever it may be.
- The more you do this, the more you will become aware, the better you will play.
- It takes practice to do this. It just doesn't happen.
- If you eliminate all the stuff on the bad side, what will happen?

ATHLETES GET IN THE ZONE AND SO DO COACHES

The "Zoooone". What is this experience that athletes and coaches talk about?

Thoughts, clear, decisive, uncluttered, confident might be the terms you would use. You might say one of the following or you might say them all.

My mind is clear.

I'm in control.

Everything works,

I'm not worried.

Things run smoothly.

Communication seems effortless.

I'm not worried about outcomes.

Things just happen.

I have self-control.

Everything is going well.

I have no fears.

Rules are followed.

I'm not frustrated or stressed.

If something goes wrong, no problem. It is easily solved.

I'm calm, positive.

I have positive emotions.

Everything comes together.

I'm focused and relaxed.

I enjoy what I am doing.

It's easy.

The zone is complete attention to the execution of a task. It is a mental state of being completely engrossed in a performance at the exclusion of everything else. When you are in the zone, you perform at your very best completely trusting your abilities. You are in complete control of your actions and reactions. You are so focused that distractions do not enter the picture. It is a state of ease that comes often to great athletes and less frequently, if at all, to those who seem to mishandle stress and distraction.

By learning and practicing concentration or focus, just like another skill, you can improve your zone probabilities.

I have often wondered if coaches ever get in the zone while they are coaching. Have you ever felt that you were in the zone during any of your coaching experiences?

What would it be like if you could be in the zone while coaching? Several coaches were asked these questions and here are some of their answers.

Dan Brooks, Head Women's Golf Coach, Duke University

When I'm coaching well or when coaching comes easily:

Given the individualistic and potentially frustrating nature of golf, a coach is sometimes tempted to opt out of the process of helping a particular player, or the entire team, take developmental steps. That is, it is easy to not coach an individual sport like golf- to play it safe and leave development entirely up to the players. Whenever I have succumbed to this temptation, I have experienced a lifeless, unrewarding feeling. However, when I am feeling effective as a coach, I never enlist such fearful, safe behavior. To the contrary, I become more involved, aware, and ready. I recognize team dynamics clearly—even sometimes predict them. I know when to act and when to sit still; and, most importantly, sitting still is *always* a calculated act—not a 'head in the sand' response. I feel in tune with my player's personalities and life situations and feel adaptable to them. Therefore, I feel adept at measuring my words, on and off the lesson tee. Humor is at my disposal as a very effective tool—and it comes easily! I somehow know when to let life itself teach a player, when to intervene, and when to help a player see that life tried to teach her something. Cultivating a sense of responsibility and ownership is, I think, a coach's most important and most difficult task: When I am feeling effective as a coach, I instinctively and gladly accept *my* responsibility to teach these skills without fear or hesitation.

Valorie Kondos, UCLA Head Gymnastic Coach
Winner of three National NCAA Championships

"The Zone" is the term of the moment for that place in time where one's senses are focused on the moment, and everything surrounding the pinpoint present has blurred to non-sensory.

I have spent the majority of my forty-two years either as a professional ballet dancer or as a gymnastics coach. While one is considered an art form, and the other a sport, both involve very similar training and preparation - mental, physical, and emotional - in order to achieve that state of performance euphoria called "The Zone". As a dancer, it was the greatest and ultimate feeling when all of my senses and synapses "clicked". I always felt it was at that moment that the music infiltrated my cells, allowing music and body to move as one. The mind wasn't a factor at that moment because it had done its job in training innumerable repetitions to meld body movement and music. Once this was achieved, whether in the dance studio or on stage, I had entered "the zone". Once in "the zone", "thought" is not only unnecessary but will more times than not break the bodies flow and rhythm disrupting the sharpness of focus.

Analyzing "the zone" from a coaching experience is quite different. The similarities include the sharpness in focus solely on that which is in your specific field of intent. The difference is training your mind to act and react versus your body. (However, I must admit, being able to stand calmly and confidently as a strong show of support and confidence while your athlete is flipping on a 4" wide beam has taken years of physical training to achieve). Whether in the training gym or competition floor, a strong focus or "zone" is achieved when all of my senses, including intuition, are working together to motivate an athlete to think, thus ultimately feel a certain way. In athletics, it isn't talent that will ultimately determine success, but the ability to achieve the desired state of mind necessary to allow the talent and training to perform to their best ability.

When asked about coaching in the zone, what comes to mind most is being on the competition floor in the heat of an event and being totally consumed with observing and reacting (or in a lot of cases, not reacting) to the movements and actions of our athletes. It is this observation supported by years of coaching (training as a coach), getting to know the small and large nuances of the athletes, and intuition that allow me to coach them affectively in the heat of the battle. It is during these times that everything around me fades to black, the cheering in the stands, the other teams competing, even the judges sitting in their blue suits ready to evaluate and assign a score. When in the zone, I have no thought as to whether we are "winning" or "losing". The unbridled and natural urge is to simply keep the moment flowing.

IN THE ZONE

The first time I was in "the zone" as a player was during the finals of a long one-day volleyball tournament in Long Beach in 1964. We had started at about 9:00am and were playing in the finals of a double elimination tournament about twelve hours later. I went up to spike a set near the left sideline and I saw the opposing middle blocker running over to block my shot. Everything slowed down and I could see his arms rise slowly above the net and his fingers spread as he made his move. The set traveled in slow motion and I found the seam between the middle blocker and pounded the ball to the floor. I can still see the expression on the middle blocker's face. After that first spike in "the zone", I saw everything in slow motion and with extraordinary clarity for the remainder of the finals.

It happened again in Czechoslovakia in 1966 when I was playing volleyball for the USA Team against China. It was a five-game match that lasted over three hours. I was in "the zone" the entire match. I saw the blockers' hands so clearly and continually hit the ball off their fingers into the stands where the defenders could not retrieve it.

Twenty years went by and I had just read *Golf in the Kingdom,* by Michael Murphy, which is a fictional account of the mystical aspects of golf in Scotland. It discussed the power of the mind in golf. My first class was at 10:30am the next day, so I decided to get up at the crack of dawn and play 18 holes before I started teaching. I drove to a local course that I was familiar with and saw that is was completely covered by a dense fog. None of the golfers ahead of me were willing to tee off until the fog lifted, so I went off first as a single. With great concentration, I played ten holes with the visibility of only twenty-five yards and did not lose my ball. At the eleventh hole, I went into "the zone". I pulled a long drive into the rough past the left side of the fairway. I pictured the ball coming to rest at the first of the three palm trees about a wedge away from the green. I walked directly to that spot and found my ball. I could not see the pin position, nor could I see the green. I hit a shot that I pictured stopping two feet left of the pin in the back of the green and then found the ball exactly where I had imagined it and tapped it in for a birdie. After that, the fog rapidly started to lift, the course became alive with golfers and I returned to my normal game of bogie golf.

In 1993, I was coaching UCLA in the NCAA Men's Finals. Halfway through the match, I knew what play the opposing setter was going to call and whom he was going to set to. I verbally relayed this information to my blockers. I did not know what play my setter was calling or whom he was going to set to unless I told him. Suddenly, I was in the mind of the opposing setter and from that point on, the other team did not have a chance.

Al Scates
Head Volleyball Coach-UCLA
Winner of 18 National Championships

FITNESS

Overall fitness is critical to golfing success. A strong and flexible body can enhance performance, endurance and consistency. Furthermore, being fit is a pre-courser to good health habits that can improve your overall health for the rest of your life. Fitness should be fun and is best done as team effort.

Exercise programs should start out slowly and be guided by experts. Universities have trained exercise personnel and special exercise facilities. Coaches should check with their trainers and have a specific program to benefit their athletes. It is important to listen to your body and not exceed pain tolerance. Professional golfers train seriously to maintain strength and endurance and gain distance. I know that by working out, freshman in college can gain 10 to 20 yards off the tee with a good exercise program. Furthermore, conditioning prevents injury. One needs to train on a regular basis. Two to three times a week allowing one day between sessions to regroup muscles. Conditioning also increases cardiovascular health as well as energy levels and reduces stress. Tests have proven that conditioning also reduces the risk of heart disease, stroke, and back pain, controls weight, and can lower a person's blood cholesterol. Cardiovascular exercise should be done thirty minutes four or five days a week.

Water

Water is essential for all sports. Water is brain food and should be consumed by athletes during competitions on a regular basis. On page 249 is a recommendation of the International Center for Sports Nutrition for the U.S. Olympic Committee Sports Medicine Division. Revised 1993.

Nutrition

Nutrition is another important consideration for athletes in any sport. Most universities have a nutritionist that advises its athletes. Nowadays it is more important than ever before to educate athletes in proper nutrition. Children in this country are gaining weight at an alarming rate, and the only reason for their excess poundage is the choices they make.

It is as simple as that.

Here are a few basic guidelines.

- Start hydrating yourself the day before competition and continue during competition.
- Eat a balanced diet.
- Do not eat fat and excessive protein before competition.
- Eat small amounts of fruit or other low sugar foods during competition on a regular basis. Have a snack every three holes.

WATER!!!
THE MOST IMPORTANT NUTRIENT

U S A

Sports Medicine Division

You could live without food for 30 days but, depending upon various conditions, you could survive only 4 to 10 days without water. Water is second only to oxygen as essential for life.

Water is without a doubt the most important nutrient for an athlete. Odd as it may sound, your body is made up primarily of water. A muscular athlete is about 70 percent water.

Body cells function best when well hydrated (have adequate water). In exercise, your muscles work extremely hard and create energy. A by-product of that energy is heat. Your body needs to get rid of the heat and, to do so, your blood circulates to the muscles, picks up the heat, and circulates to the top of the skin. Sweating takes place, you lose water, it evaporates, cooling the blood and in turn the blood circulates back again and the process is repeated. It's similar to the cooling system of a car.

TRAINING OR COMPETING

When training or competing, you can lose a lot of water by sweating... which must be replaced to perform your best. Losing as little as two to three percent of your body weight by heat can cause a decrease in concentration, coordination, strength, and stamina.

You should drink at least eight glasses (two liters) of water a day. During heavy physical activity you will need to drink more. Some athletes lose three to five liters of water... more in hot, humid weather.

If you sweat off one pound, this is equal to a half-liter (two cups of water). You should drink water before, during, and after practice or competition. Keep an eye on the scale for weight changes. Weigh-in nude before and after the activity and be guided accordingly.

RISKS OF DEHYDRATION

If the water you lose through sweat is not replaced, blood volume decreases. In the milder forms of heat illness, dizziness or fainting may occur. If you continue to exercise unaware of the symptoms, the sweating mechanism can shut down. If this happens, normal body temperature will rise. Heat stroke can follow.

Heat stroke is the most serious form of heat illness. Death can result if critical areas of the brain are damaged due to high body temperature. Replacing the water you lose is essential.

Don't take salt tablets. Water will be pulled into the stomach to dilute the salt so it can be absorbed. If the team physician believes extra salt is needed, it should be added to meals or through salty foods such as ham, pizza, nuts and chips.

HOW MUCH?

There is no single answer to "How much water do I need?" It varies among athletes and depends on the situation. Some athletes don't sweat much, and body temperature is maintained even in hot weather. Others are "heavy sweaters." They may drop from 8 to 10 pounds during a competition or practice session.

A heavy sweater will lose more water by sweating and consequently will need to replace more. (One pound body weight = 1/2 liter of water). So, the weigh-in, weigh-out process will provide the formula.

MYTHS

Myths about drinking water during training or competition are rampant. Some of the more frequently heard myths are:

"Taking water prior to exercise will cause stomach cramps."

"Working out in the heat without water makes you tough."

"Drinking water before competition will make you waterlogged."

It has been proven that consuming water, even in large amounts, prior to and during activity has no adverse effects on performance.

Water is the life-blood of an athlete. Keep it flowing for the best performance. The importance of water cannot be overstated.

Prepared by the International Center for Sports Nutrition for the U.S. Olympic Committee Sports Medicine Division - Revised 1993.

CHAPTER VII

Conclusion

THE WILL TO WIN

If you want a thing bad enough
To go out and fight for it,
Work day and night for it,
Give up your time and your peace and
       your sleep for it,
If only desire of it
Makes you quite mad enough
Never to tire of it,
Makes you hold all other things tawdry and
       cheap for it,
If life seems all empty and useless without it
And all that you scheme and dream
       is about it,
If gladly you'll sweat for it,
Fret for it,
Plan for it,
Lose all your terror of God or man for it,
If you'll simply go after that thing that
       you want
With all your capacity,
Strength, and sagacity,
Faith, hope, and confidence,
       Stern pertinacity,
If neither cold poverty, famished and gaunt,
Nor sickness nor pain
Of body and brain
Can turn you away from the thing that
       you want,
If dogged and grim you besiege and beset it,
       You'll get it.

Berton Braley

WHETHER YOU THINK YOU
CAN AND OR YOU CAN'T
YOU'RE PROBABLY RIGHT

If you think you are beaten, you are;
If you think that you dare not, you don't
If you'd like to win, but you think you can't,
It's almost certain you won't.

If you think you'll lose, you've lost;
For out in the world you'll find
Success begins with a fellow's will.
It's all in the state of mind.

If you think you are outclassed, you are;
You've got to think high to rise;
You've got to be sure of yourself before
You can ever win a prize.

Life's battles don't always go
To the stronger or faster man;
But sooner or later the man who wins
Is the man who thinks he can.

"I'm the greatest. I said that even before I knew I was. Don't tell me I can't do something. Don't tell me it's impossible. Don't tell me I'm not the greatest. I'm the double greatest."

Mohammed Ali

Believe in yourself. Believe in your team. Talk like a champion.
Walk like a champion. Act like a champion. Practice like a champion.
And sooner or later you will be a champion.

More Something to Think About

When I am playing good and driving straight, I can't wait until the next tournament. It's gratifying to know you can do what you have to do in order to win. And it's a lot easier to do well when you're enjoying it, when you are having fun.

Johnny Miller

It's great to win, but it's so great fun just to be in the thick of any truly well and hard-fought contest against opponents you respect, whatever the outcome.

Jack Nicklaus

Do not let what you cannot do interfere with what you can do.

John Wooden

Show me a guy who's afraid to look bad and I'll show you a guy you can beat every time.

Lou Brock

I'm a great believer in luck and the harder I work, the more I have of it.

Thomas Jefferson

The way a team plays as a whole determines its success. You may have the greatest bunch of individual stars in the world, but if they don't play together, the club won't be worth a dime.

Babe Ruth

A winner never whines.

Paul Brown

You have to be important. Anyone that has patience in coaching won't be successful or isn't going to be around long. It is easy to talk about waiting around three to five years to rebuild and coming out a better team on the other end. But you have to lose while you're rebuilding. Usually losing comes with patience.

John Madden

It's like wrestling a gorilla. You don't quit when you're tired, you quit when the gorilla is tired.

Robert Strauss

When you become aware of what it takes to get to the next level, you're on your way.

Team competition is fun. It is the love of the battle, and the thrill of working toward a goal with your teammates.

With enough practice golf clubs can be turned into magic wands.

The following materials are examples of drawings, lessons, forms and examples written by athletes. Use them as you wish or create your own.

QUESTIONAIRRE
Evaluation/Golf GPA

Scale A,B,C,D,F

1. I would rate my golf accomplishments this year.   A B C D F
2. I would rate the team accomplishments this year.   A B C D F
3. My attitude this year during tournament play was very good.   A B C D F
4. My cooperation this year was great. (Uniform, meals, on time, rules)   A B C D F
5. My enthusiasm to participate was great during practice and in tournaments.   A B C D F
6. My participation in the final assignment was good. (Affirmations)   A B C D F
7. I <u>really</u> got done with my swing, alignment, set up, and grip for Nationals.   A B C D F
8. My team spirit was great.   A B C D F
9. The team's spirit was great.   A B C D F
10. My listening skills were good. (Willingness to listen).   A B C D F
11. I was willing to do something different. (Risk)   A B C D F
12. I was tolerant.   A B C D F
13. I was thoughtful.   A B C D F
14. I was appreciative.   A B C D F
15. I was open minded.   A B C D F
16. I was giving.   A B C D F
17. I anchored my good shots.   A B C D F
18. I was dispassionate with my bad shots.   A B C D F
19. I did my routine before <u>every</u> shot in practice.   A B C D F
20. When I practiced, I changed something after I hit a good shot. (Target, club, distance, etc.)   A B C D F
21. I resisted hitting just one more shot after hitting a good shot.   A B C D F
22. I always went over the course in my mind before each tournament round.   A B C D F
23. I always analyzed my stats in order to find out what to practice.   A B C D F
24. My equipment is correct.   A B C D F
25. I worked on my short game 75% of my practice time.   A B C D F
26. My nutritional habits were good.   A B C D F
27. When there was a problem on the team, I always tried to solve it.   A B C D F
28. I set a good example always.   A B C D F
29. I felt I could talk to coach about (circle)   Personal problems
                                                            Team problems
                                                            Golf game
30. I would like to talk to coach more about: (list)

257

EVALUATION FORM

1. There is a clear and shared vision of why the team exists
2. The team has well defined goals.
3. Priorities are understood and agreed to.
4. There is little waste of time.
5. Risk and unacceptable outcomes (results) are accepted and learned from.
6. Team members help each other routinely.
7. Problems are solved efficiently and effectively.
8. Team is appreciative and satisfied.
9. Team members treat each other with integrity and dignity.
10. Responsibility is understood.
11. Team is congenial and comfortable.
12. Conflicts and differences are accepted, valued, and confronted.
13. Team leadership keeps team focused.
14. There is confidence in each others commitment and ability.
15. People talk to each other clearly and frequently.
16. People listen to each other for understanding.
17. Feedback is sought.
18. Team sees itself as working together.
19. Team sees itself as winners.
20. Team and individual growth occurs.
21. Team members give 100%.
22. Team members are interested in finding the best way as opposed to having their own way.
23. Team is loyal.
24. Team acts, talks, looks and walks like winners.
25. Team members use practice times efficiently.
26. Team members are enthusiastic and willing to do what is asked of them.
27. Team members are adaptable.
28. Team has fun.

HIGH PERFORMING TEAM RATING FORM

How would you rate your team? Put a number between 1 and 5 by each statement. One being the lowest and 5 being the highest.

Purpose:
1. ___Team members can describe and are committed to a common purpose.
2. ___Goals are clear and challenging.
3. ___Strategies for achieving goals are clear.
4. ___Individual roles are clear.

Empowerment:
1. ___Members feel a personal and collective sense of power.
2. ___Members have access to necessary skills and resources.
3. ___Policies and practices support team objectives.
4. ___Mutual respect and willingness to help each other is evident.

Relationships:
1. ___Members express themselves openly and honestly.
2. ___Compassion, understanding and acceptance are expressed.
3. ___Members like to listen to each other.
4. ___Differences of opinion and perspective are valued.

Adaptability:
1. ___Members share responsibility for team leadership and team development.
2. ___Members are adaptable to changing demands.
3. ___Various ideas and approaches are explored.

Productivity:
1. ___Efficient practice is evident.
2. ___Quality of practice or play is excellent.
3. ___Clear problem solving is apparent.

Recognition and Appreciation:
1. ___Individual contributions are recognized and appreciated by leader and other members.
2. ___Team accomplishments are recognized by members.
3. ___Group members feel respected.
4. ___Team contributions are valued and recognized by the coach.

Morale:
1. ___Individuals feel good about their membership on the team.
2. ___Individuals are confident and motivated.
3. ___Members have a sense of pride and satisfaction about their ability and play.
4. ___There is a strong sense of cohesion and team spirit.

Near the end of the year speech-

"You want to be successful these last two tournaments. Right? You have worked hard the whole year and you all deserve to do well. Right? Here is a plan for you for the next couple of weeks.

Prepare for Regionals by dreaming every night how you will play, how you will swing, chip, pitch, sand-wedge (?) and putt, and how much fun you will have. In your dreams walk through the door that you colored last week, leading to the first tee, and see yourself in competition. Get involved with the colors you see, the feel of the wind, the warmth of the sun and the sounds you hear. Experience the feel of good shots, the sensation of the ball going into the hole. Use your imagination. Hover over the golf course like a helicopter and picture each hole, or fly like a butterfly, and inspect each pin placement. Be a little green man in the bottom of the cup ready to catch the ball. Pretend you are an arrow that zings at the bull's eye. Be a camera that sees all, or maybe a feather or a cloud floating over the tee, or a rainbow ending in the cup. You can even be a piece of cotton that slowly carries your ball softly onto the green and close to the cup. You can get so involved with how wonderfully you will be playing, how happy you will be and how much fun you will be having that, automagically, wonderful things will happen during the real tournament. You could even see yourself and the team at the end of the tournament standing in front of everybody as the winners. Feel what that will feel like. Picture what you will be wearing and how you will be smiling and what you will be saying. The whole experience could actually happen. Wouldn't that be absolutely magnificent? Wouldn't you be happy, excited and up? Go for it. What can you lose? You have a week to dream about Regionals and three weeks to dream about Nationals. Dreams do come true for deserving and wonderful people like you."

I wonder, how many times Tiger dreamed about the Master's?

Something to think about again!

If you always do what you've always done, you'll always get what you've always got.

If something is not working for you, do something different. Anything! It is crazy to do the same thing over and over again and expect different results.

Have a definite preshot routine that you do before every shot, putter through driver. The preshot routine sets you up for a good shot. It is the same for every club in your bag. It is something you do without thinking before you hit a shot on the golf course or on the driving range. It takes discipline. Golf is all about discipline.

Positive thinking is the only way. You can't afford any negative thoughts on the golf course. So if you say or think, I can't putt today, or my driver isn't working, or my rhythm is off, or my swing isn't working today, guess what? It won't. You are sending your brain a clear message and believe me your brain is a smart customer. It will do whatever you request. It doesn't care if it is right or wrong, good or bad.

Potential minus interferences equals your performance. Therefore, when you are playing golf, your attention must be on the shot at hand. Thinking about the people ahead who are slow, your mechanics, or what your are going to have for dinner are interferences that can prevent you from making a good shot.

Ask for what you want. You will get it. Remember the brain doesn't recognize don't or not. So if you say aloud or even think, "Don't go in the water", guess what? Your brain says, "Yes master, we go in the water." End of story. So always, ask for what you want. I want this ball to go in the hole. I want this ball to land on the green. Your chances are a hundred times better.

It isn't what you say that counts. It is what you do that counts. It's true in golf and in life. Stop trying and start doing. Try trying less. When you are in the trying mode, performance is questionable. It is like fear. Fear prevents you from accomplishing your goal. Fear stands in your way. Therefore, if you are afraid you'll miss a putt, afraid you'll top the ball, afraid you'll succeed or fail, you are done. **DONE! Get it?**

In college golf, the coach usually sends to the new recruits and the returning team members information concerning the coming year which includes the schedule, rules, updates, *etc.* The following is a sample of a summer bulletin. High school coaches could also consider adapting this bulletin for their team members.

19 -19

COACH STEINMANN

UCLA WOMEN'S GOLF TEAM

TABLE OF CONTENTS

1. LETTER - NEWS
2. ROSTER OF TEAM MEMBERS AND COACHES
3. TOURNAMENT SCHEDULE
4. OPEN HOUSE FOR PARENTS AND TEAM MEMBERS
5. MAP TO COACH'S HOUSE
6. TEAM GUIDELINES
7. GENERAL TEAM RULES
8. PHYSICAL FITNESS
9. QUALIFYING RULES
10. RULES FOR COUNTRY CLUBS
11. ATTITUDE DETERMINES APTITUDE
12. WORDS OF WISDOM
13. ENCLOSURES:
    FITNESS GUIDE FOR SUMMER
    SCHOOL CALENDAR

July 4,

Dear Team,

Have been running around the world. Had a great time in Sweden. Saw Amanda in Copenhagen and Mia in Lund. Saw two Junior Tournaments in Sweden, and the seminar with the Swedish Coaches was really good. I learned some new techniques and new ways of looking at what we do, but it was interesting to find out that we do a lot of the same things.

I am on my way to Oregon for a few days and then to Wyoming to see my son and his family. At the end of July, I will be giving a seminar to Coaches in Philadelphia just before the USGA Junior which I will watch for a few days. Then it's home for the month of August to get ready for the new season.

I hope you are having a good summer so far and getting some needed rest and relaxation. Keep me posted on the tournaments you play and how you're doing. I watch the paper, but sometimes I miss the results.

Physicals will be on September 9 at 1:00 PM. We leave for our first Tournament on September 22.

Give my best regards to your parents.

Coach

Golf Team Members and Coaches

Name and Year   Address   Phone

List your students.

Coach Jackie Tobian-Steinmann

1998-1999 WOMENS GOLF SCHEDULE

DAYS	DATE	TOURNAMENT	LOCATION
FALL			
	9/24 to 9/26	**NEW MEXICO**	Albuquerque, NM
	10/5 to 10/7	**PREVIEW**	Tulsa, OK
	10/23 to 10/25	**STANFORD**	Palo Alto, CA
	11/1 to 11/3	**HAWAII**	Kauai, Princeville, HI
WINTER			
	2/8 to 2/10	**REGIONAL CHALLENGE**	Palos Verdes, CA
	3/21 to 3/24	**PIONEER-ELECTRONIC**	Temecula, CA
SPRING			
	3/12 to 3/14	**LSU**	Baton Rouge, LA
	4/2 to 4/4	**ASU**	Phoenix, AZ
	4/10 to 4/11	**STANFORD**	Palo Alto, CA
POST SEASON			
	4/19 to 4/21	**PAC 10**	Stanford, Palo Alto, CA
	5/16 to 8 ?	**REGIONALS**	Texas Tech, Lubbock, TX
	5/19 to 5/22	**NCAA'S**	Tulsa, OK

SEPTEMBER 13

4 PARENTS AND
TEAM

COACH'S
HOUSE

HOLLYWOOD

3:00 PM
to
4:30 PM

GENERAL TEAM RULES:

1. You are expected to attend a team meeting once a week when scheduled.

2. Being on time, grooming, looking and acting like a winner is important to your coaches. We represent UCLA.

3. You are responsible for obtaining yardage books for tournaments. You should have one for every practice course we play. Buy a few empty small notebooks that will fit in your pocket. Keep all yardage books in a shoe box for subsequent years.

4. Alcohol, smoking, drugs are not allowed. Violation can mean immediate dismissal from the team.

5. If you want to discuss something with me individually and privately, you may always do so in my office or hotel room at tournaments. If you are sick, let me know so that I can assist you.

6. Tutoring: If you must cancel your tutoring appointment because of a tournament or other problem, it is your responsibility. Two appointments missed and you are out of tutoring for the remainder of the year. Call and cancel when you must. **The department is charged when you don't show up. Do not schedule professor sessions, appointments, tutors, etc., during team meetings or practice time.**

7. Weight training: *See separate sheet.*

8. Participation in recruiting is the responsibility of every member of the team.

9. At times we are asked to do community service, i.e. appearing at tournaments and participating in a closest-to-hole contest, etc. Please do your share when asked. Also it is mandatory to be at the Friends of Golf preparations for their tournament.

10. Parents and friends are welcome at tournaments and may join us for dinner. The team eats together.

11. NCAA rules:

    Universities are not allowed to pay for personal calls from hotel rooms.

    Shorts must be no shorter than 4 inches above the knee.

    Parents and spectators must remain 15 yards from you at tournaments.

RULES OR GUIDELINES FOR UCLA TEAM

This year you will make the rules for the team at the first meeting. Start jotting down what you think is important for the UCLA team to consider when setting guidelines. Be able to say after each guideline, "will be best for the team, or will help us play better, or will assist us in our daily life, or assist us in the future."

Consider some of the following:
Nutrition
Weight training
Practice
Tournaments
Respect
Responsibility
Yardage books
Feedback
Team meetings
Etc.

Qualifying

Playing in tournaments is a privilege as well as a way to experience the joy of competition and a chance to strive together as a group. Junior tournaments and college tournaments are held all over the United States and the world. Qualifying is a way to determine the participants.

The lowest scores count.

However, having said that, sometimes there are considerations. In college the coach may exempt a player from qualifying because of their performance in the previous tournament. Also, an athlete may be prohibited from qualifying because of academic or behavioral problems. Each coach has his or her own rules. Hopefully they are fair, clear and consistent.

RULES FOR COUNTRY CLUBS

HILLCREST
Park to far left.
Always check with starter.
No practice area or range.
Shorts no shorter than 4" above the middle of the knee.
Shirts with collars.

MT. GATE
Before you tee off check with the starter.
Shorts at proper length.
Tokens are $2.50 each. A big bucket is $5.00. Don't waste the balls. UCLA pays for the balls.
Save some balls to use on the chipping green.
You may wear pants.
Collared shirts.
No member should have to wait for a space on the range or around the chipping green.
Chip and putt 3 or 4 at a time. Not all of you.

RIVIERA
Range to use is the far section on the day we play there.
Shorts or pants allowed. Shorts must be proper length.
Every other Tuesday.
Putting on green OK.
Short game area can be used if no members present.
Can hit a few drivers on the regular range area before play if not full.

BEL AIR
Park in lower lot.
Can't walk across entry area in golf shoes.
Use distinguishable shoe bag and put street shoes in bag above lockers in the ladies' locker room.
Play in threesomes.
Fix your ball mark and one or two others.
Kick divots in or carry a sand bag.
No jeans. Shorts must be just a little above the knee.

BRENTWOOD
Must park in stall at far end.
Don't walk across greens with bag.
Place flagstick on fringe.
Put clubs and yourself in caddie area.
Do not putt on putting green or use the range.
Only go to tee when it is your group's time to tee off.
Kick divots in.
Shorts proper length or pants.

WILSHIRE CC
Same rules apply. Shorts the proper length, etc.

PALOS VERDES CC
Same rules.

We represent UCLA. It is a privilege to play these courses. It may seem as if we are second class citizens at times, but we must overlook that. We cannot risk losing the courses we play on. If you break a rule or one of your teammates breaks a rule, you are jeopardizing our privilege. Remind your teammates, it is your responsibility. There is to be no tobacco or alcohol on the course obviously. Please dress clean and neat and in the proper golf attire so that there is no question from any member.

ATTITUDE DETERMINES APTITUDE

ATTITUDE
1. The team takes priority over the individual.
2. Go about your daily tasks in a cheerful and purposeful manner.
3. Proper attitude consists of the will to win, eagerness to learn and the intelligence to use what you've learned.
4. Give instead of take.

DISCIPLINE
1. Doing what needs to be done to the best of your ability consistently.
2. Self discipline and desire will sometimes compensate for ability.
3. Every great player has spent hours and hours practicing her weak points.
4. Individuals who practice self-discipline (not just say they practice self-discipline) improve their game. It's not what you say that counts, it's what you do that counts.
5. Keeping physically fit takes self-discipline.
6. Practicing with a purpose takes discipline.
7. Discipline yourself to make good choices in golf and in your life.
8. Discipline yourself to always do your routine with every shot or putt.
9. Discipline yourself to follow one of the laws of golf...When working on mechanics, no target...When there is a target, no mechanics.
10. Discipline yourself to always practice making putts.
11. Discipline yourself to work on your mental routine as well as your physical routine.
12. Discipline yourself to find fun and enjoyment in every shot you make no matter what the outcome.
13. Discipline yourself to build a library in your brain of good shots by getting emotionally attached to your good shots and dispassionate with your bad shots.
14. Discipline yourself to keep a notebook of what you sense in every round you play.
15. Winners are self-disciplined. Discipline yourself to do what winners do.

RESPECT
1. Your actions will reflect a picture of you and the team. Act accordingly.
2. Demonstrate honesty and loyalty towards your teammates, coaches and other individuals associated with UCLA.
3. Accept your coaches' criticism in the spirit it is intended. When a coach ceases to correct your mistakes, then you have cause to worry.

PRIDE
1. Demonstrate the privilege of playing for UCLA.
2. Encourage your teammates.
3. Recognize successes of teammates.
4. The best players help others to become better players.
5. Decide to win. Develop a burning desire to give all you've got in order to be the best. Be persistent.
6. Act like a winner, look like a winner, talk like a winner.
7. Stop sweating over the small stuff.
8. Become your vision, and accomplish your goals.
9. Winners give 100% effort in everything they do.

All the above are choices by the way........

WORDS OF WISDOM

Know what you want, and act as if you already have it.

Dedication and commitment lead to success.

Team spirit makes it fun.

A smile warms the heart.

Golf is only a game.

When something is fun, you enjoy doing it.

You have the talent and the tools to be the best.

Make UCLA #1

EXAMPLES TO USE IN LESSONS

The following drawings, cartoons and forms are some ideas that I have used. You can copy them or make your own. It just takes some imagination and a pen Give the athletes a box of crayons or colored pens and have them decorate. Once they have permission to imagine, they will have fun, and listen attentively to your lesson. When their masterpiece is finished, have them post it on their bathroom door so that they see it every day. What they think about comes about.

DANGEROUS SITUATION - One prolonged horn blast (MUST stop immediately)
NON-DANGEROUS SITUATION - Several short intermittent blasts

Resumption Signal _____ _____
Two prolonged horn blasts.

Hole placements are measured in paces.

277

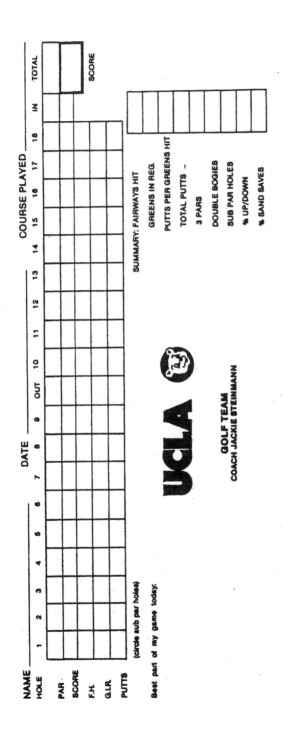

NAME
DATE
COURSE PLAYED

HOLE	1	2	3	4	5	6	7	8	9	OUT	10	11	12	13	14	15	16	17	18	IN	TOTAL
PAR																					
SCORE																					
F.H.																					
G.I.R.																					
PUTTS																					

(circle sub par holes)

Best part of my game today:

SCORE

SUMMARY: FAIRWAYS HIT

GREENS IN REG.

PUTTS PER GREENS HIT

TOTAL PUTTS –

3 PARS

DOUBLE BOGIES

SUB PAR HOLES

% UP/DOWN

% SAND SAVES

UCLA

GOLF TEAM
COACH JACKIE STEINMANN

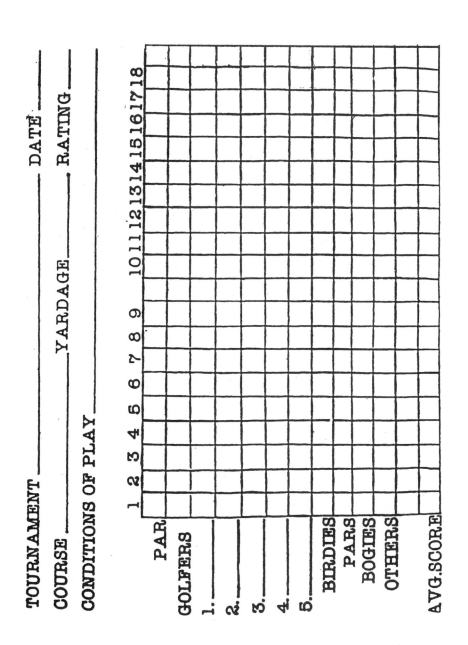

TOURNAMENT _____ DATE _____

COURSE _____ YARDAGE _____ RATING _____

CONDITIONS OF PLAY _____

	1	2	3	4	5	6	7	8	9	10	11	12	13	14	15	16	17	18
PAR																		
GOLFERS																			
1.																			
2.																			
3.																			
4.																			
5.																			
BIRDIES																			
PARS																			
BOGIES																			
OTHERS																			
AVG.SCORE																			

CLASS INFORMATION SHEET

Name .... Campus Address ....

Campus Phone No. .... Home Address ....

Home Phone No. .... Major .... Year in School ....

Shoe Size .... Soc. Sec. No. .... Sport ....

Term .... Year ....

NO. OF CREDIT HOURS	COURSE & TITLE	DEPT.	NO.	TLN	HOUR	DAY	RM.	BLDG.	INSTRUCTOR

	MONDAY	TUESDAY	WEDNESDAY	THURSDAY	FRIDAY	SATURDAY	SUNDAY
7:30							
8:30							
9:30							
10:30							
11:30							
12:30							
1:30							
2:30							
3:30							
4:30							
5:30							
6:30							
7:30							
8:30							
9:30							

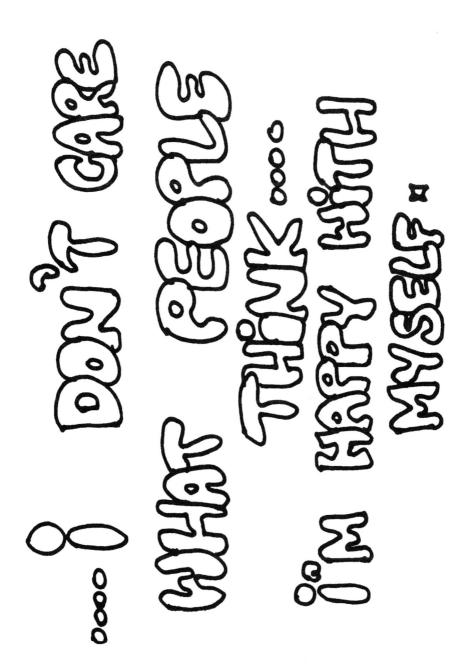

POTENTIAL – INTERFERENCE

EQUALS

PERFORMANCE

List interferences:

i.e.: • IS THIS THE RIGHT CLUB
• WHAT'S FOR DINNER
• WHO IS WATCHING
• WHAT IF I MISS.....

THERE IS NO BAD ME, JUST BAD SHOT RESULTS.

NO GUILT, THREAT, ANXIETY OR INTIMIDATION.

THERE IS JUST THE NEXT SHOT.

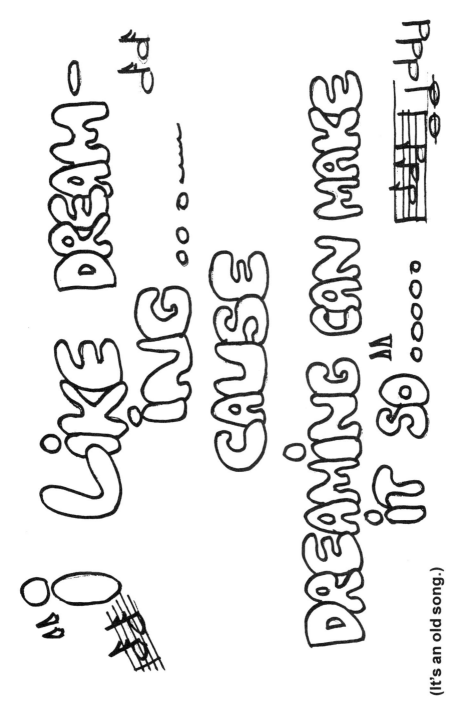

(It's an old song.)

I AM A GREAT PUTTER :)

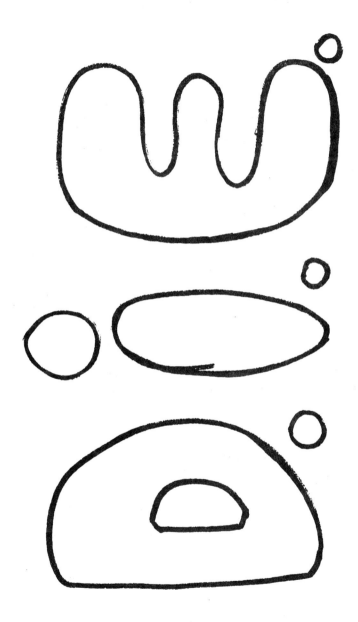

DISTANCE is EVERYTHING

IMAGINE HOW YOU CAN DO IT AND EVENTUALLY YOU CAN

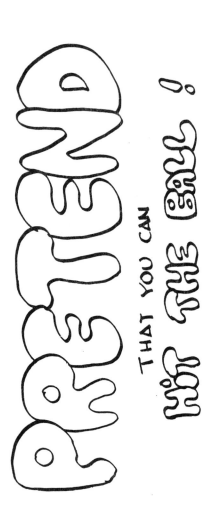

THAT YOU CAN

HIT THE BALL !

M.C.

PRETEND LONG ENOUGH AND YOU BECOME WHAT YOU PRETEND.

FAKE IT TILL YOU MAKE IT !

...ACT AS THO YOU HAVE PERSONAL POWER AND KNOW WHAT TO DO....

C.H.

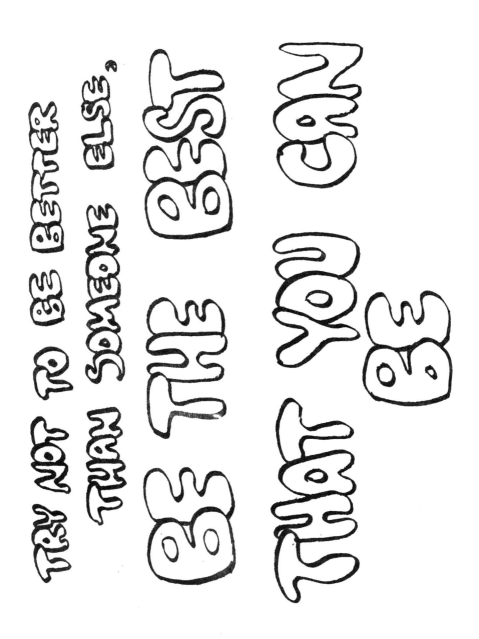

TRY NOT TO BE BETTER THAN SOMEONE ELSE, BE THE BEST THAT YOU CAN BE

GOLF IS FUN

From "Golf is Fun" by SANDRA EGGERT

63% OF MY SCORE SHORT : ARE SHOTS

FANTASY PROVIDES ACCOMODATION TO A PURPOSE OR FUNCTION.

A CHILD BONDED TO ANXIETY
CAN NOT HELP BECOMING ANXIOUS.

→

BURN OUT

←

OVER COACHED YOUNGSTERS, THE GAME CRAMMED "DOWN THEIR THROAT", PARENTS OR LITTLE LEAGUE COACHES WHO, THEMSELVES, ARE ANXIOUS.

"PROJECTION"

"72 73 73 73"

I AM A SCORING MACHINE

In the game of golf, the only important thing is getting the ball in the hole. It doesn't matter how I do it

.... and finally, This is what really matters. The rest is all #&*$@!
.... As coaches, teachers and parents, you must be willing to...

- Remain inquisitive and imaginative.
- Be receptive to new ideas.
- Be experimental and adaptable.
- Laugh and have fun.
- Have energy and passion about what you do.
- Be truthful.
- Be loving.
- Enjoy learning.
- Venture into the unknown.
- Challenge your limitations.
- Get out of the way of learners and let them learn.
- Not allow your wants to interfere with the wants and motives of others.
- Be a model. Be what you want them to be.
- Be self-worthy so that others will be also.
- Be a good listener and observer so that you can understand others.
- Have unconditional love and acceptance of others.
- Have rules that are clear, concise and fair.
- Follow the Golden Rule.

Everybody loses when we have the opportunity to seek a better way, and we do nothing. Everybody wins doing the above. It's not what you say that counts. It's what you do. "Keep doing the doing."

CONCLUSION

Life is a blast and so are golf, coaching and teaching. There are many challenges to solve on an everyday basis. That is what life is all about. Often we take ourselves too seriously and get involved with little things that really are not important. Sometimes we may lose our ability to imagine and create and, in the process, lose the energy to be effective. We forget about the big picture.

Take care of yourself. Recognize and appreciate the good things in your life and your accomplishments. Count your blessings and understand that disappointments are only an opportunity to achieve something better.

Above all, have fun. Nurture a sense of humor. Fall in love with teaching, coaching and golf. Nothing will ever be perfect, so enjoy what you do. Keep your perspective. Realize, in the long run, that you are a very lucky person to have what you have and do what you do. You have a great responsibility in shaping the future of everyone you touch.

My best to all you.

Jump out of bed every morning and yell,

"I get to coach today," or

"I get to play golf today," or

"I get to teach today!"

Do it everyday and you will be surprised at the results.

Contributors
Bibliography
Suggested Readings

Contributor List

1. Mark Lasch, Golf Stat
2. Renee Baumgartner, Ph.D, S.W.A.D. and Former Golf Coach, University of Oregon
3. Therese Hesion, Golf Coach, Ohio State University, Former LPGA Tour Player
4. Heidi Steinmann, Consultant
5. Carrie Leary, Golf Coach, UCLA, former UCLA Golf Team Member
6. Chuck Hogan, Golf Teacher, Coach, Author and Mentor
7. Dan Brooks, Golf Coach, Duke University, Winner of 1 National Championship
8. John Wooden, Basketball Coach, UCLA (Ret.), Winner of 10 National Championships
9. Al Scates, Volleyball Coach, UCLA, Winner of 18 National Championships
10. Kenny Sheba, Golf Teacher, Club Fitter
11. Valorie Kondos, Gymnastics Coach, UCLA, Winner of 3 National Championships

Addtional illustrations courtesy of:
United Media
Warner Brothers
King Features
Hanna-Barbera

Editor: Mary Bishop
marybishop@zianet.com

Bibliography and Suggested Reading

The Achievement Zone, Shane Murphy
Extraordinary Golf, Fred Shoemaker
Quantum Golf, Kjell Enhager
The Golf of Your Dreams, Dr. Bob Rotella
Introduction to NLP, O'Connor and Seymour
Learning Golf, Chuck Hogan
Practicing Golf, Chuck Hogan
Be Your Own Best Coach, Pia Nillsson
The Mental Art of Putting, Cohen and Winters
Ageless Body Timeless Mind, Deepak Chopra
Aim to Win, Chuck Hogan
Building High Performing Teams, Ken Blanchard
Chicken Soup, Jack Canfield
Conversations with God, Neale Walsch
Five Days to Golfing Excellence, Chuck Hogan
Freedom from Fear Forever, James Durlacher
Leadership, Ken Blanchard
Magical Child, Joseph Chilton Pearce
Mental Toughness Training for Sports, James Loehr
Neuro-Linguistic Programming, Joseph O'Connor and John Seymour
Players Course, Chuck Hogan
Quantum Healing, Deepak Chopra
Smart Moves
The Magic of Thinking Big, David Schwartz
The One Minute Manager, Ken Blanchard
Twelve Means to Lower Scores, Chuck Hogan
The Edge

Playing the Great Game of Golf, Ken Blanchard

Wooden, Coach John Wooden with Steve Jamison

Golf is Not a Game of Perfect, Dr. Bob Rotella

The Golf of Your Dreams, Dr. Bob Rotella

Golf Is a Game of Confidence, Dr. Bob Rotella

And if you Play Golf, You're My Friend, Harvey Penick

Rethinking Golf, Chuck Hogan

Golf and the Intelligence of Play, Athletics and the Intelligence of Play, Inc.

Magical Parent Magical Child, Michael Mendizza with Joseph Chilton Pearce

On a personal note, I am adding a letter written by my daughter.

It is the type of letter every mother should get.

Jacqueline Ann Steinmann
April 3rd, 1997
On The Occasion of Her 70th Birthday

Birthdays are a celebration of the birth of a life, and as that life grows and gains dimension through life experiences, a birthday becomes a celebration of the person that life has become. I can't think of many lives that I would want to celebrate more than yours.

I admire you as a person, I cherish you as a friend, and I love you as a Mother.

I love your passion and enthusiasm. When you commit, you jump in with every ounce of your being. Whether it's a Christmas soufflé, a new golf philosophy, a new assignment as Director and President of just about anything, or a quest to better mankind, you go for it, Mom. Your passion and enthusiasm combined with your high standards of excellence make you an outstanding leader with results that speak for themselves. Your energy and enthusiasm is contagious, it rubs off on everyone around you. I love that about you. You set a shining example for those who follow. Just by being in it, you make the world a better place.

As a friend, you are always there when I need you, even if you're on the other side of the world (which you usually are during three weeks of every month). We talk about everything, and you listen well. We laugh. We're silly. We try to figure out how we can change the world. Or we can be together without saying a word. You know me better than anyone and I don't have to pretend to be anyone other than myself. That's a friend!

As a mother myself, I know how much you cherish your children. You've done a wonderful job raising all of us. I know now how difficult that had to have been, and how much work it took. And I also know that you wouldn't have traded it for anything in the world, because for the many times raising any of us caused you pain, we brought you three times as much joy...a kind of joy you can't get anywhere else. Thank you for being my Mother, for your care and for your unconditional love. And you know, the other thing about you that never seizes to amaze me is your generosity. It knows no bounds. You're an amazing woman, Mom.

I love you, Mom,
You're the best Mother on Earth,
You're my best friend,
You're my hero and inspiration!

Happy 70th Birthday, From Your Daughter Heidi

UCLA National Champion Coach
National Coach of the Year
Pac 10 Coach of the Year
LPGA Coach of the Year
Hall of Fame Coach